PHILIP'S

C000127013

Cycle TOURS

The Peak District

Gordon Selway

First published in 2002 by
Philip's, a division of
Octopus Publishing Group Ltd
2-4 Heron Quays
London E14 4JP

First edition 2002
First impression 2002

Based on the original Ordnance Survey Cycle Tours series
first published by Philip's and Ordnance Survey®.

ISBN 0-540-08206-6

The route maps in this book are reproduced from
Ordnance Survey® Landranger® mapping.

Text and compilation copyright © George Philip Ltd 2002

This product includes mapping data licensed from Ordnance
Survey® with the permission of the Controller of Her Majesty's
Stationery Office. © Crown copyright 2002. All rights reserved.
Licence number 100011710

Photographic acknowledgements

AA Photo Library 25, 31, 36, 44, 48, 66, 112 • Derek Forss 7,
22, 55, 61, 67, 95, 106, 116 • Judy Todd 78, 85, 91, 99

Contents

Abbreviations and symbols

Directions

L	left
R	right
LH	left-hand
RH	right-hand
SA	straight ahead or straight across
T-j	T-junction, a junction where you have to give way
X-roads	crossroads, a junction where you may or may not have to give way
'Placename 2'	words in quotation marks are those that appear on signposts; the numbers indicate distance in miles unless stated otherwise

Distance and grade

The number of drink bottles indicates the grade:

🍾 Easy
🍾🍾🍾 Moderate
🍾🍾🍾🍾🍾🍾 Strenuous

The grade is based on the amount of climbing involved.

Refreshments

Pubs and teashops on or near the route are listed. The tankard 🍺 symbols indicate pubs particularly liked by the author.

Page diagrams

The page diagrams on the introductory pages show how the map pages have been laid out, how they overlap and if any inset maps have been used.

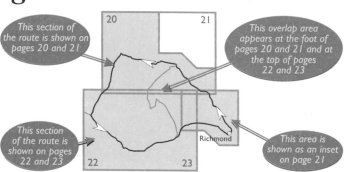

This section of the route is shown on pages 20 and 21

This overlap area appears at the foot of pages 20 and 21 and at the top of pages 22 and 23

This section of the route is shown on pages 22 and 23

This area is shown as an inset on page 21

Richmond

20 21 22 23

Cross-profiles

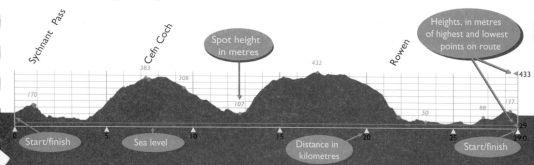

Sychnant Pass
Cefn Coch
383
308
170
Spot height in metres
107
432
Rowen
Heights, in metres of highest and lowest points on route
433
137
88
50
29
Start/finish
Sea level
Distance in kilometres
Start/finish
0 5 10 15 20 25 29.0

Legend to 1:50 000 maps

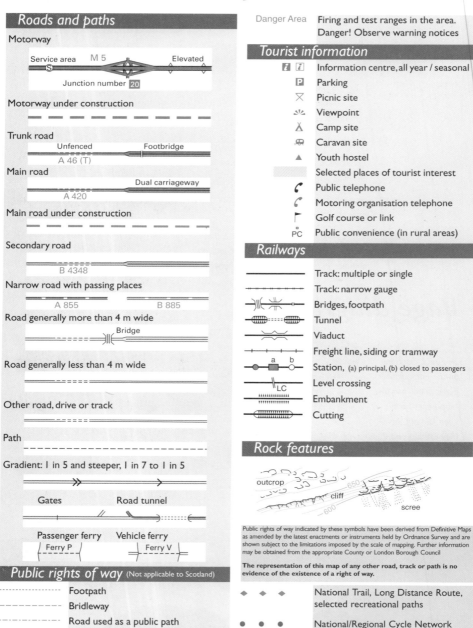

Roads and paths

Motorway

Service area   M 5   Elevated
S
Junction number 20

Motorway under construction

Trunk road
Unfenced   Footbridge
A 46 (T)

Main road
Dual carriageway
A 420

Main road under construction

Secondary road
B 4348

Narrow road with passing places
A 855   B 885

Road generally more than 4 m wide
Bridge

Road generally less than 4 m wide

Other road, drive or track

Path

Gradient: 1 in 5 and steeper, 1 in 7 to 1 in 5

Gates   Road tunnel

Passenger ferry   Vehicle ferry
Ferry P   Ferry V

Public rights of way (Not applicable to Scotland)

--------- Footpath
--------- Bridleway
-·-·-·-·- Road used as a public path
-+-+-+-+- Byway open to all traffic

Danger Area Firing and test ranges in the area.
Danger! Observe warning notices

Tourist information

🄸 🄸	Information centre, all year / seasonal
P	Parking
✕	Picnic site
☼	Viewpoint
🏕	Camp site
🚐	Caravan site
▲	Youth hostel
	Selected places of tourist interest
☎	Public telephone
☎	Motoring organisation telephone
⌐	Golf course or link
PC	Public convenience (in rural areas)

Railways

——————— Track: multiple or single
——·——·—— Track: narrow gauge
Bridges, footpath
Tunnel
Viaduct
Freight line, siding or tramway
a   b
Station, (a) principal, (b) closed to passengers
LC Level crossing
Embankment
Cutting

Rock features

outcrop
650
cliff
600
scree

Public rights of way indicated by these symbols have been derived from Definitive Maps as amended by the latest enactments or instruments held by Ordnance Survey and are shown subject to the limitations imposed by the scale of mapping. Further information may be obtained from the appropriate County or London Borough Council

The representation of this map of any other road, track or path is no evidence of the existence of a right of way.

◆ ◆ ◆   National Trail, Long Distance Route, selected recreational paths

● ● ●   National/Regional Cycle Network
— — —   Surfaced cycle route

Water features

Canal (dry)
Canal
Aqueduct
Lake
Weir
Towpath
Lock
Ford
Footbridge   Bridge
Normal tidal limit
Marsh or salting

Slopes
Cliff
Flat rock
Sand Dunes
High water mark
Low water mark
Lighthouse (in use)
Lighthouse (disused)
Mud
Beacon
Shingle

General features

Electricity transmission line (with pylons spaced conventionally)

Pipeline (arrow indicates direction of flow)

ruin   Buildings

Public buildings (selected)

Bus or coach station

Coniferous wood

Non-coniferous wood

Mixed wood

Orchard

Park or ornamental grounds

Quarry

Spoil heap, refuse tip or dump

Radio or TV mast

Church or chapel with tower

Church or chapel with spire

Church or chapel without tower or spire

Chimney or tower

Glasshouse

Graticule intersection at 5' intervals

Heliport

Triangulation pillar

Windmill with or without sails

Windpump

Boundaries

National

London borough

National park or forest park

NT   National Trust

NT   open access

NT   limited access

County, region or islands area

District

Abbreviations

P   Post office
PH   Public house
MS   Milestone
MP   Milepost
CH   Clubhouse
PC   Public convenience (in rural areas)
TH   Town hall, guildhall or equivalent
CG   Coastguard

Antiquities

VILLA   Roman

Castle   Non-Roman

Battlefield (with date)

Tumulus

Position of antiquity which cannot be drawn to scale

Ancient monuments and historic buildings in the care of the Secretaries of State for the Environment, for Scotland and for Wales and that are open to the public

Heights

50   Contours are at 10 metres vertical interval

·144   Heights are to the nearest metre above mean sea level

Heights shown close to a triangulation pillar refer to the station height at ground level and not necessarily to the summit

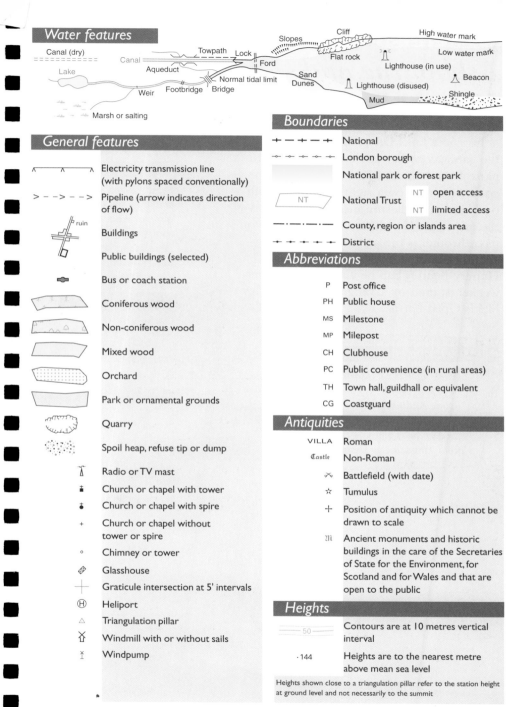

Kedleston, Ashbourne and Hungry Bentley

*T*his route links Derby with Ashbourne, the gateway to Dovedale and the western part of the National Park but it is also a good ride in its own right. The house and parkland at Kedleston merit a visit, but for the most part it is the countryside that you pass through is the main attraction. The site of the deserted medieval village of Hungry Bentley can be visited on summer weekends (and by arrangement) at Bentley Fields Open Farm.

Start

Derby Station

P As above

Distance and grade

51 km (32 miles)

Easy/moderate

Terrain

Mostly lowland with short climbs on the outward section of the route including one quite steep climb out of Ashbourne over about 200 m (yd)

Nearest railway

Derby

Refreshments

Plenty of choice in **Derby**
Kedleston Hall Refreshment Room, **Kedleston**
Plenty of choice in **Ashbourne**
(Several pubs on route back from Ashbourne to Derby)

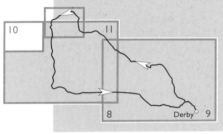

▶ *Kedleston Perk*

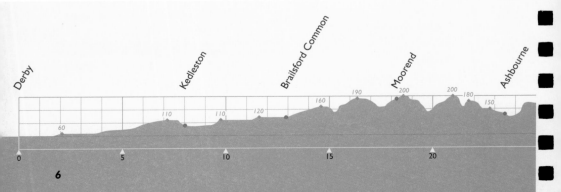

Derby 1

A busy city and a centre of our remaining railway industry with much of interest, often down side streets or away from the centre. The City Museum and Art Gallery has, among other things, an excellent collection of paintings by Wright 'of Derby', a magnificent collection of Crown Derby porcelain and displays on the old Midland Railway

Kedleston Hall 5

A magnificent Georgian stately home, with extensive gardens, parkland and serpentine lake. Owned by the National Trust and open to the public on most summer afternoons

Ashbourne 14

One of the gateways to the Peak at the lower end of Dovedale and the old market centre of west Derbyshire. There are many attractive buildings of the 18th and 19th-centuries. On Shrove Tuesday and Ash Wednesday each year, a medieval football game (with the goals several kilometres apart) is played

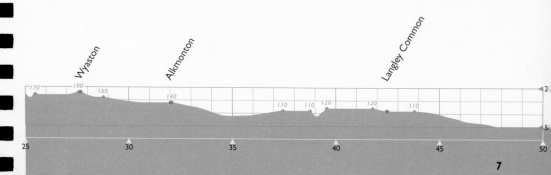

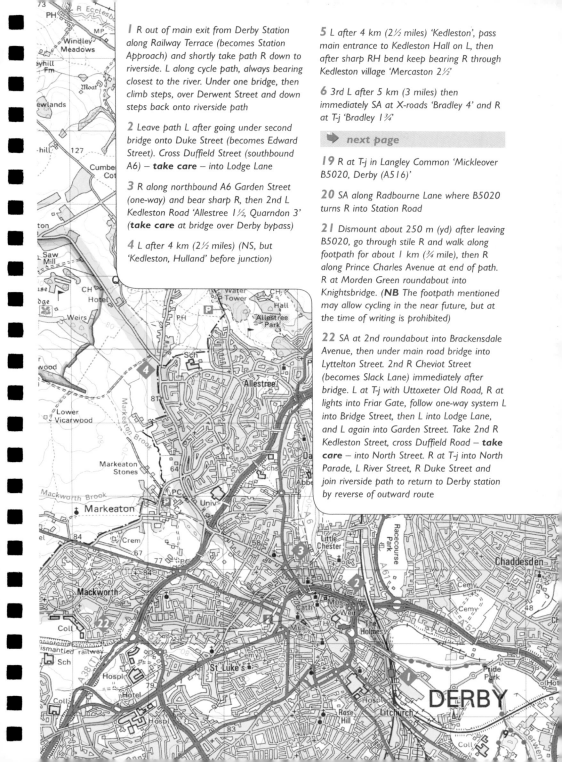

1 R out of main exit from Derby Station along Railway Terrace (becomes Station Approach) and shortly take path R down to riverside. L along cycle path, always bearing closest to the river. Under one bridge, then climb steps, over Derwent Street and down steps back onto riverside path

2 Leave path L after going under second bridge onto Duke Street (becomes Edward Street). Cross Duffield Street (southbound A6) – **take care** – into Lodge Lane

3 R along northbound A6 Garden Street (one-way) and bear sharp R, then 2nd L Kedleston Road 'Allestree 1½, Quarndon 3' (**take care** at bridge over Derby bypass)

4 L after 4 km (2½ miles) (NS, but 'Kedleston, Hulland' before junction)

5 L after 4 km (2½ miles) 'Kedleston', pass main entrance to Kedleston Hall on L, then after sharp RH bend keep bearing R through Kedleston village 'Mercaston 2½'

6 3rd L after 5 km (3 miles) then immediately SA at X-roads 'Bradley 4' and R at T-j 'Bradley 1¾'

➤ **next page**

19 R at T-j in Langley Common 'Mickleover B5020, Derby (A516)'

20 SA along Radbourne Lane where B5020 turns R into Station Road

21 Dismount about 250 m (yd) after leaving B5020, go through stile R and walk along footpath for about 1 km (¾ mile), then R along Prince Charles Avenue at end of path. R at Morden Green roundabout into Knightsbridge. (**NB** The footpath mentioned may allow cycling in the near future, but at the time of writing is prohibited)

22 SA at 2nd roundabout into Brackensdale Avenue, then under main road bridge into Lyttelton Street. 2nd R Cheviot Street (becomes Slack Lane) immediately after bridge. L at T-j with Uttoxeter Old Road, R at lights into Friar Gate, follow one-way system L into Bridge Street, then L into Lodge Lane, and L again into Garden Street. Take 2nd R Kedleston Street, cross Duffield Road – **take care** – into North Street. R at T-j into North Parade, L River Street, R Duke Street and join riverside path to return to Derby station by reverse of outward route

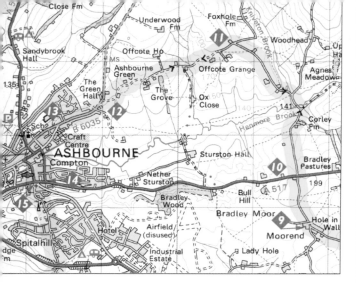

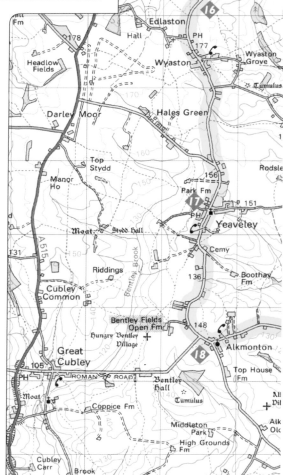

7 L after 4 km (2½ miles) 'Bradley ½'

8 L (NS), then L again at T-j and shortly 1st R (in effect SA) onto Hadley Lane 'Moorend ½'

9 R at T-j after 800 m (½ mile) 'Ashbourne 2½' and immediately through Hole in the Wall

10 **Take care** – SA at X-roads with A517 'Offcote, Kniveton'

11 L at T-j 'Ashbourne 2'

12 Obliquely L at T-j with B5035 'Ashbourne'

13 Fork L 'Town Centre, Derby A52', then L again after 400 m (¼ mile) Park Road

14 R at T-j with A517 'Town Centre A52'

15 2nd L at traffic lights Old Hill (NS, one-way street) uphill past Plough PH and SA, going under Ashbourne bypass in about 1 km (¾ mile)

16 R at T-j after 2½ km (1½ miles) 'Edlaston, Wyaston'

17 R (in effect SA) between church and PH in Yeaveley

18 L in Alkmonton 'Longford, Kirk Langley' continuing along Long Lane for about 10½ km (6½ miles)

← *previous page*

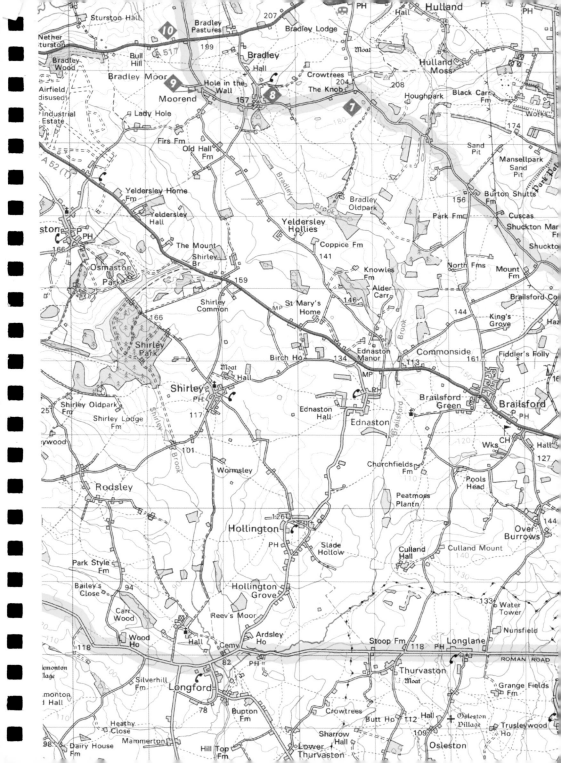

The Churnet Valley and Somersal Herbert

A day's on-road ride through the contrasting countryside south of the White Peak visiting the Churnet Valley and the uplands of southwest Derbyshire where there are extensive views in fine weather. The steep-sided, wooded valley of the River Churnet has been called Staffordshire's Switzerland and there are many enjoyable walks through the woods around Oakamoor.

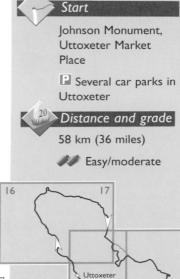

Start

Johnson Monument, Uttoxeter Market Place

P Several car parks in Uttoxeter

Distance and grade

58 km (36 miles)

Easy/moderate

Refreshments

Plenty of choice in **Uttoxeter**
Pubs in **Stramshall, Hallington, Oakamoor, Ellastone** and **Roston**
Crown Inn, **Marston Montgomery**
Shop and PH in **Church Broughton**
Tea room at Sudbury Hall, **Sudbury**
Dog and Partridge PH, **Marchington**

1 Ride away from kiosk side of Johnson Memorial in Uttoxeter Market Place and fork R at roundabout by Three Tuns PH (Ashbourne B5033)

2 SA at roundabout with A50 – **take care** – busy trunk road, B5030 'Rocester, Ashbourne'

3 1st L 'Spath ¼'

 four pages

15 L at T-j (offset X-roads) after 4 km (2½ miles) 'Thurvaston 1, Marston 1, Cubley 2¾' and fork R 'Marston Montgomery ¾'

16 2nd R in Marston Montgomery (Somersal Lane, 'Somersal Herbert 2½') after Crown Inn (**Or** continue SA here and pick up directions after 4 km (2½ miles) from instruction 22)

17 Easy to miss – R after 2½ km (1½ miles) gated road (NS) – if you pass Somersal House on left you have gone too far

18 L at T-j in Somersal Herbert 'Sudbury 2'

19 L at T-j beside chapel 'Marston Montgomery'

20 R after 800 m (½ mile) – in effect SA (NS)

two pages

33 R in Marchington (NS) shortly after Dog & Partridge PH into Hall Lane, bear L

34 R Moisty Lane (NS)

35 R after 5 km (3 miles) at T-j with B5017 (NS) cross railway line, then 2nd L to return to Uttoxeter Market Place

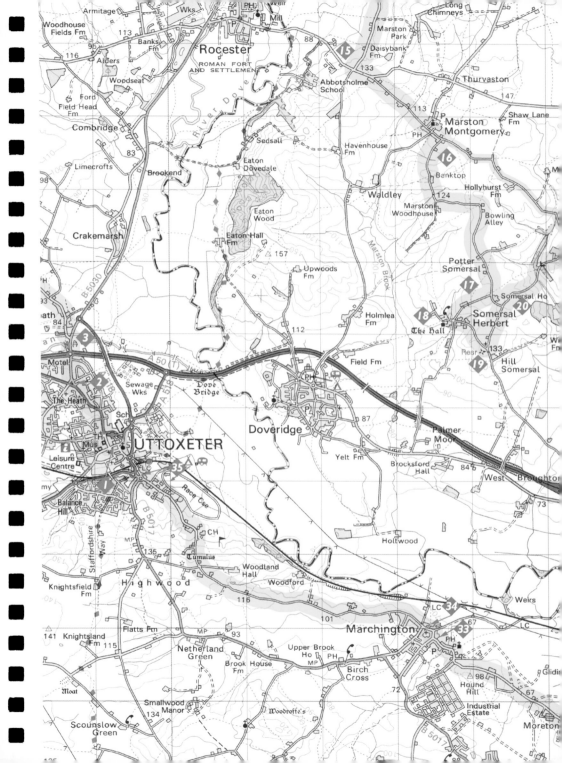

Places of interest

Uttoxeter 1

A modest country town with strong dairying and pastoral connections. It also has links with Samuel Johnson, compiler of the first English dictionary in the 1750s. His father sold books in the market here and Samuel refused to take his place when requested. He returned to do penance years later and the event is still commemorated each September

Alton Towers 11

A spectacular, early 19th-century mansion in Tudor style (part demolished) with formal gardens. Now, the grounds house one of the country's major tourist attractions, the Alton Towers leisure park. Pugin (who contributed to the Palace of Westminster) was one of a series of architects employed by the Earls of Shrewsbury to realize their dream here

Terrain

Woodland to the west of the River Dove but otherwise open country. Climbs to Hallington and past Threapwood and short climbs out of Oakamoor and leaving Somersal Herbert. A fairly long but easy ride

Nearest railway

Uttoxeter

21 R at T-j 'Sudbury 3'

22 R at T-j 'Lichfield A515, Sudbury', then immediately L 'Boylestone, Church Broughton'

23 R at T-j 'Sapperton, Church Broughton'

24 L at X-roads after 1 km (¾ mile) 'Church Broughton 1'

25 SA at X-roads Church Road

26 R opposite church (NS)

27 2nd R (NS)

28 L at T-j Cote Bottom Lane (NS)

29 L at T-j and L again before A564, then bear R at roundabout, cross dual carriageway bypass, R again at 2nd roundabout, and L 'Scropton' (not shown on map)

30 R at triangular T-j in Scropton 'Sudbury 2', Leathersley Lane

31 L at T-j 'Lichfield A515; Draycott-in-the-Clay 2½, King's Bromley 10'

32 R after 2½ km (1½ miles) Moreton Lane 'Moreton'

➡ two pages

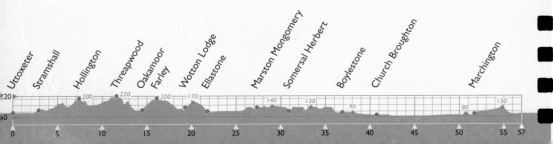

4 R by church in Stramshall, Hollington Lane (NS)

5 L at T-j 'Tean 3, Cheadle 4', then R 'Tean 3½, Cheadle 4½' and bear R again (NS) just before church

6 R 'Great Gate ¾, Alton 2½' just after village hall on left

7 L at T-j 'Tean, Cheadle', then bear R 'Threapwood'

8 SA Chapel Lane at staggered X-roads with B5032

9 R at T-j with B5417 in Oakamoor (NS)

10 1st R after crossing River Churnet (NS)

11 R at T-j in Farley 'Alton', then L (in effect SA) Wootton Lane 'Ellastone 3½' passing entrance to Alton Towers

12 R after 4 km (2½ miles) 'Prestwood 1, Denstone 2', then immediately bear sharp L

13 R at T-j with B5032 in Ellastone (NS), then 1st L Dove Street 'Norbury ¾ B5033'

14 1st R in Norbury after crossing River Dove and former railway bridge (NS). Continue through Roston

15 L at T-j (offset X-roads) after 4 km (2½ miles) 'Thurvaston 1, Marston 1, Cubley 2¾' and fork R 'Marston Montgomery ¾'

◀ *four pages*

16

3 *Staffordshire Moorlands*

A ride through remote and enchanting countryside, with a diverse past, visiting several highlights as you explore the hills, ridges and valleys of the Staffordshire part of the National Park. The route twice crosses the county boundary into Derbyshire around Hartington and follows the west bank of the River Dane in Cheshire. The end of the ride winds through the impressive Roaches and their accompanying outcrops that form the foreground to the superb view from Morridge, across the Cheshire Plain, soon after leaving Leek.

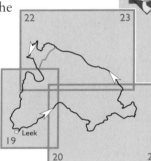

Start

Tourist Information Centre, Stockwell Street/Market Place, Leek

P Plenty in Leek

Distance and grade

48 km (30 miles)

🚴🚴🚴 Moderate

Terrain

Some long climbs from Leek to the Mermaid Inn and from Longnor to Axe Edge. Shorter climbs to Butterton and out of Wolfscote Dale. The route round Three Shire Heads is off-road and takes some effort (see on-road alternative from instruction 25)

Nearest railway

Stoke-on-Trent (16 km (10 miles) SW of Leek)

Refreshments

Plenty of choice in **Leek**
Mermaid Inn, **Morridge**
Shop and PH in **Butterton**
Manifold Valley Hotel, **Hulme End**
Plenty of choice in **Hartington** and **Longnor**   Flash Bar Shop on A53 at **Quarnford**

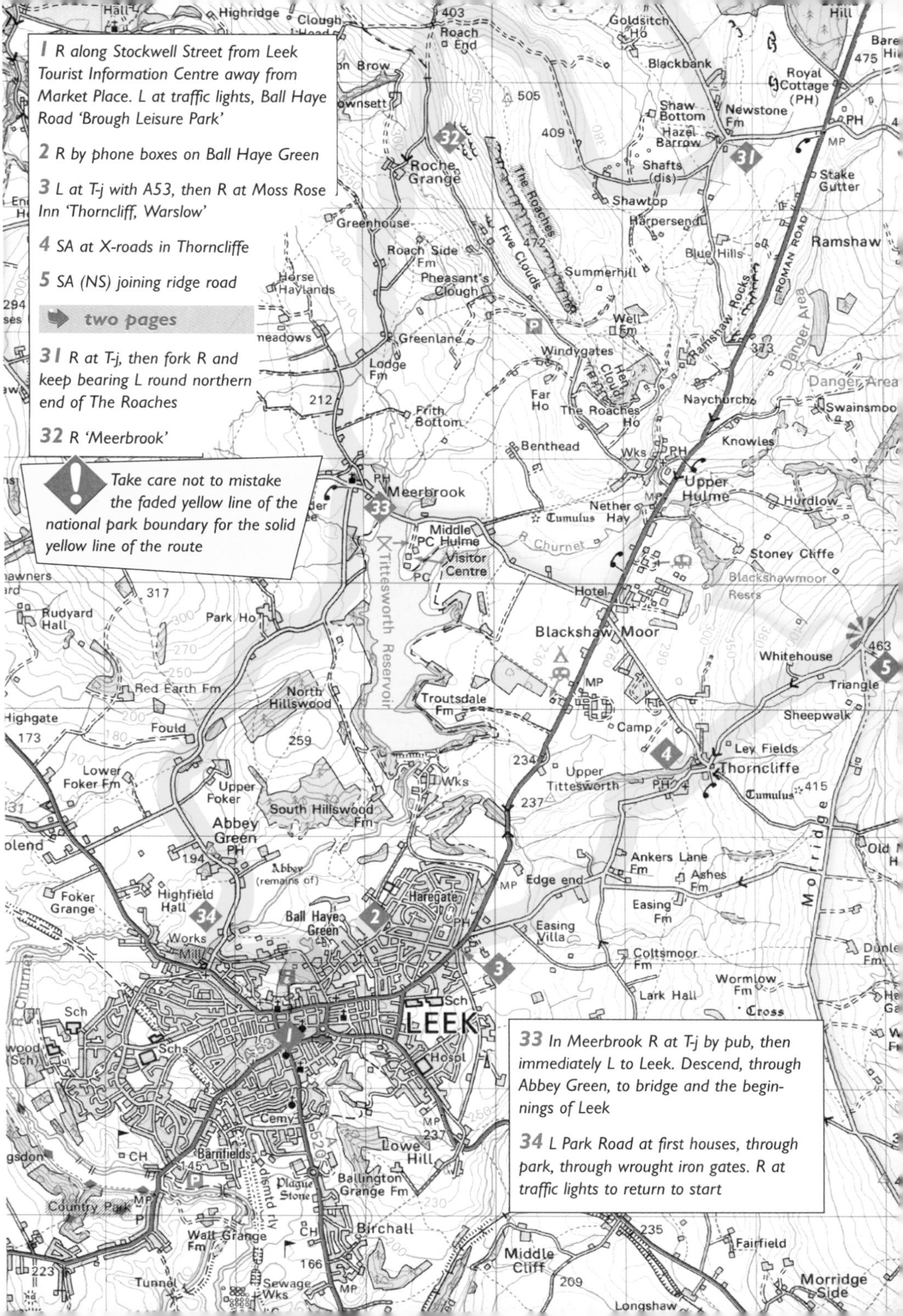

1 R along Stockwell Street from Leek Tourist Information Centre away from Market Place. L at traffic lights, Ball Haye Road 'Brough Leisure Park'

2 R by phone boxes on Ball Haye Green

3 L at T-j with A53, then R at Moss Rose Inn 'Thorncliff, Warslow'

4 SA at X-roads in Thorncliffe

5 SA (NS) joining ridge road

➡ **two pages**

31 R at T-j, then fork R and keep bearing L round northern end of The Roaches

32 R 'Meerbrook'

⚠ Take care not to mistake the faded yellow line of the national park boundary for the solid yellow line of the route

33 In Meerbrook R at T-j by pub, then immediately L to Leek. Descend, through Abbey Green, to bridge and the beginnings of Leek

34 L Park Road at first houses, through park, through wrought iron gates. R at traffic lights to return to start

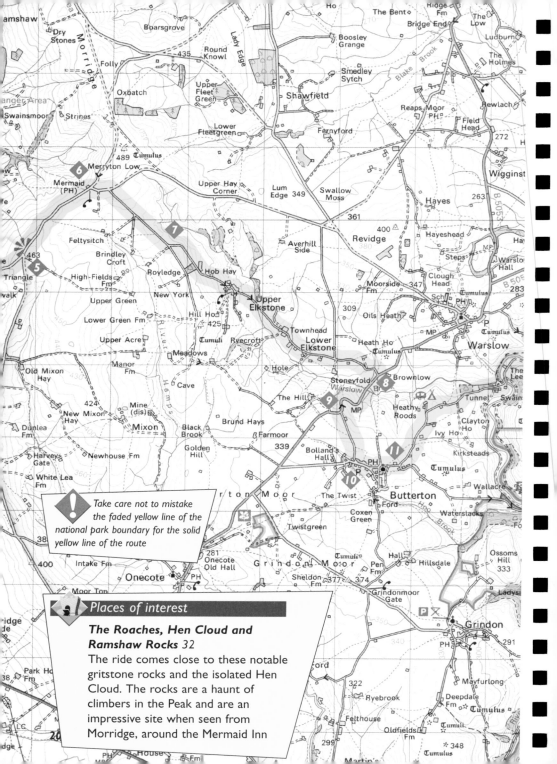

Take care not to mistake
the faded yellow line of the
national park boundary for the solid
yellow line of the route

Places of interest

The Roaches, Hen Cloud and Ramshaw Rocks 32

The ride comes close to these notable
gritstone rocks and the isolated Hen
Cloud. The rocks are a haunt of
climbers in the Peak and are an
impressive site when seen from
Morridge, around the Mermaid Inn

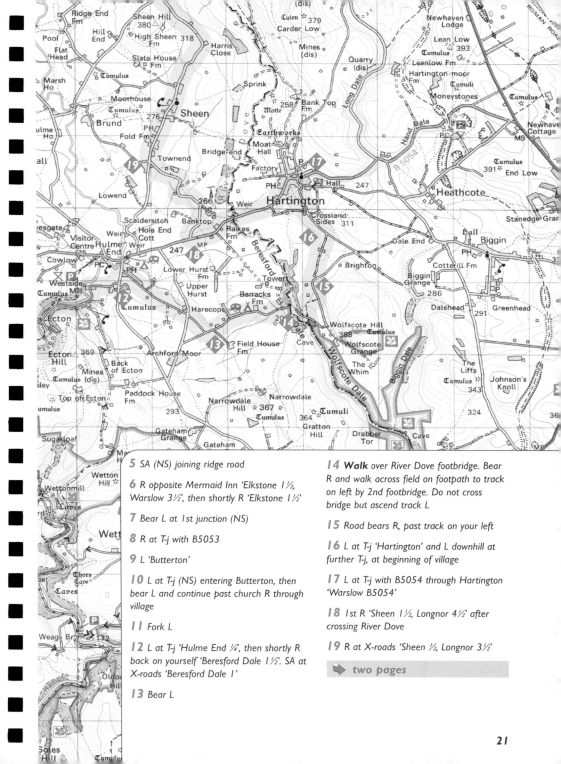

5 SA (NS) joining ridge road

6 R opposite Mermaid Inn 'Elkstone 1½, Warslow 3½', then shortly R 'Elkstone 1½'

7 Bear L at 1st junction (NS)

8 R at T-j with B5053

9 L 'Butterton'

10 L at T-j (NS) entering Butterton, then bear L and continue past church R through village

11 Fork L

12 L at T-j 'Hulme End ¼', then shortly R back on yourself 'Beresford Dale 1½'. SA at X-roads 'Beresford Dale 1'

13 Bear L

14 *Walk* over River Dove footbridge. Bear R and walk across field on footpath to track on left by 2nd footbridge. Do not cross bridge but ascend track L

15 Road bears R, past track on your left

16 L at T-j 'Hartington' and L downhill at further T-j, at beginning of village

17 L at T-j with B5054 through Hartington 'Warslow B5054'

18 1st R 'Sheen 1½, Longnor 4½' after crossing River Dove

19 R at X-roads 'Sheen ½, Longnor 3½'

➡ two pages

▲ *The Roaches from Hen Cloud*

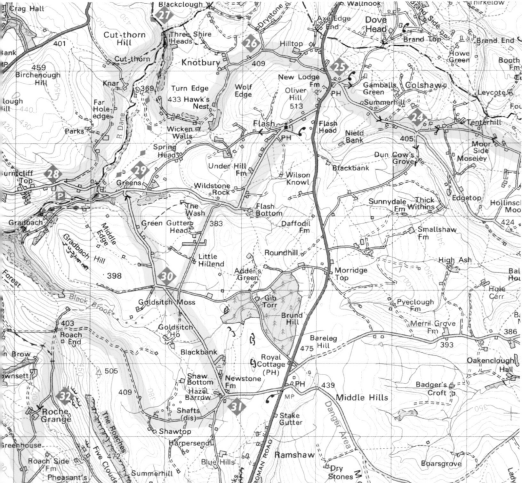

20 L at oblique T-j 'Longnor ¼, Leek 11'

21 R at X-roads in Longnor 'Buxton 6½ B5053, then 2nd L 'Hollinsclough 2, Flash 4½'

22 1st R 'Hollinsclough 1¼'

23 SA in Hollinsclough and up steep road 'Unsuitable for motors'

24 R at grass triangle T-j after 2½ km (1½ miles)

25 R at T-j with A53, then immediately L 'Knotbury 1' (**Or** L onto A53 then 1st R through Flash, then L soon after sharp RH bend. SA at X-roads, then bear L)

26 Bear L, then sharp L at drive to Knotbury Lee Farm. Go down track in valley bottom; in about 800 m (½ mile) follow track as it bears R and contours round through almost 180° in about 1 km (¾ mile), to valley head with the track fence/wall on left. Bridleway joins obliquely on left

27 Cross bridge, below the confluence of two streams, at Three Shire Heads. L sharp back on yourself on bank of River Dane and follow rough track climbing the west side of the valley to tarmacked road. L back on yourself at T-j with metalled road, then descend steeply to sharp RH bend and contour for about 1 km (¾ mile)

28 L back on yourself at T-j

29 R 'Royal Cottage 2¾, Leek 7¼'

30 Sharp bend L, then fork R

31 R at T-j, then fork R and keep bearing L round northern end of The Roaches

32 R 'Meerbrook'

Take care not to mistake the faded yellow line of the national park boundary for the solid yellow line of the route

4 The Goyt Valley and Macclesfield Forest

A notable exploration of the millstone grit country between Macclesfield and Buxton, visiting the quiet villages of Pott Shrigley and Kettleshulme, and the wilder countryside of the Goyt Valley, Axe Edge and Macclesfield Forest. The first section of the route, along the Middlewood Way, has a good tarmac surface with several gateways to negotiate and one light-controlled road crossing.

Start

Macclesfield Town Hall

P Several public car parks in Macclesfield

Distance and grade

50 km (31 miles)

Moderate/ strenuous

Terrain

Few level sections, however, you ride down most of the sharpest hills. The main climbs are from Bollington to Brink Farm, from Kettleshulme to Old Nick, up the Goyt Valley and into Macclesfield Forest

Nearest railway

Macclesfield

Refreshments

Plenty of choice in **Macclesfield**
Pubs in **Bollington**
Cosy tea rooms and pubs in **Kettleshulme**
Shop in **Quarndon** and PH in **Flash**
Pubs in **Allgreave** and **Wildboarclough**

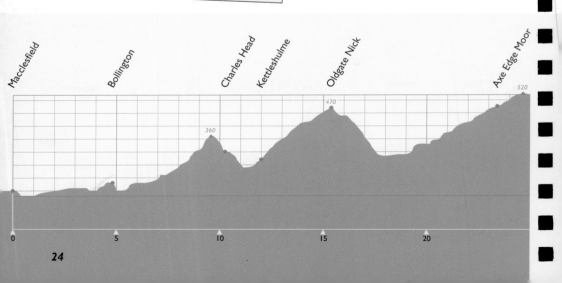

Macclesfield 2

The centre of the English silk industry for over two hundred
years from 1768, one of the mills survives as a museum of silk.
Nearby are Gawsworth Hall to the south and Adlington Hall
to the north, both 15th-century, timber-framed
houses

Flash, Gradbach and Lud's Church 15/16

Flash claims to be the highest village in England and
wears a weathered aspect. At Gradbach, a former silk
mill is now a youth hostel, while at Lud's Church
there is a deep, narrow gorge where religious dis-
senters assembled over 500 years ago. The gorge may be the
green chapel of the medieval, Arthurian work *Sir Gawain and the
Green Knight*

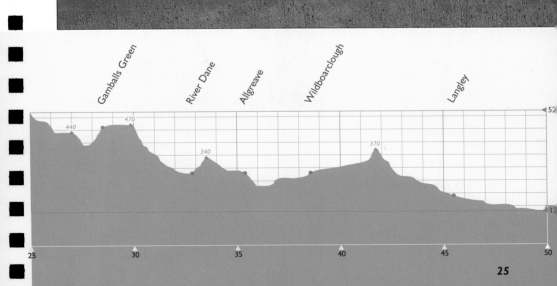

1 Facing outwards from the main entrance to Macclesfield Town Hall, turn R, then R again at traffic lights into Hibel Road and descend to roundabout. Take 2nd exit (in effect SA)

2 Pass entrance to supermarket, then L and go through gateway on left (adjoining exit from supermarket) to join Middlewood Way. After about 2 km (1¼ miles), the Middlewood Way crosses the A523 Silk Road dual carriageway

3 After a deviation L to go round a yard built across the old railway route (on foot) R at T-j with Grimshaw Lane and pass under aqueduct

4 L Chancery Lane where road bears R, then bear L North Street

5 R Shrigley Road 'Pott Shrigley, Whaley Bridge'

6 R Barkstonedale in Pott Shrigley 'Kettleshulme 3, Whaley Bridge 5'

7 L at T-j 'Kettleshulme, Whaley Bridge B5470'

8 R 'Goyt Valley 3'

9 L at T-j 'Buxton 5' and though gate in 2 km (1¼ miles) keeping reservoir on your left

10 R at T-j at head of Goyt Valley , then immediately L (NS)

11 SA at X-roads across A537 (NS), then L and immediately R to cross the A54 (NS) and over Axe Edge Moor

➡ **three pages**

19 L after 6 km (3¾ miles) 'Forest Chapel ¾ and SA at top of hill 'Langley 2½'

20 Bear R in Langley

21 Bear R in Sutton Lane Ends 'Macclesfield 2'

22 R at T-j with A523

23 R at traffic lights into Sutherland Road, continuing past railway station on R, bear R under railway line, then L at T-j, L again at roundabout and at traffic lights to enter Jordangate and return to start

Take care not to mistake the faded yellow line of the national park boundary for the solid yellow line of the route

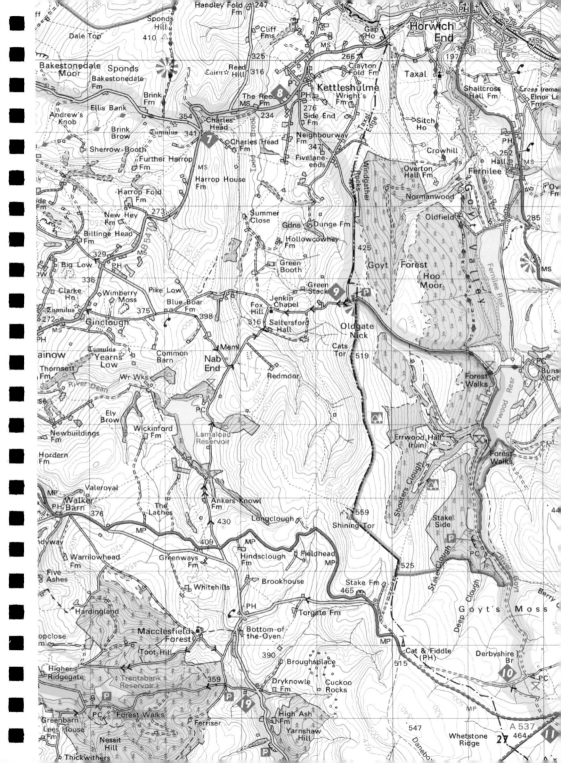

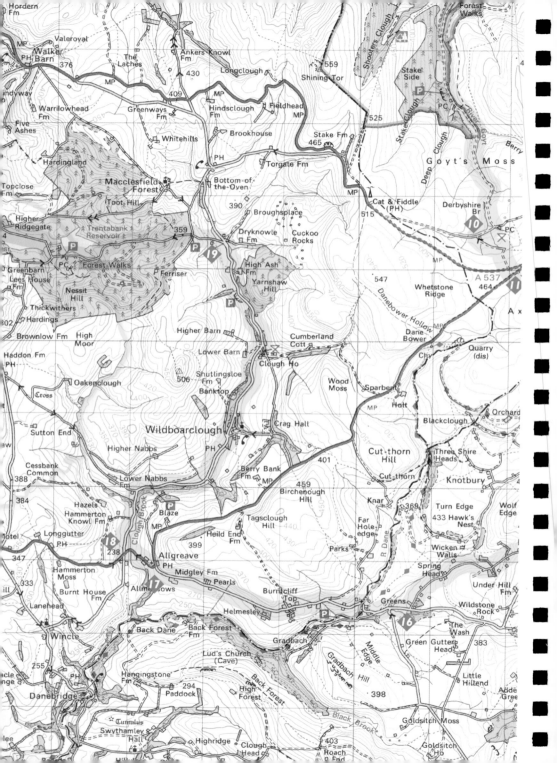

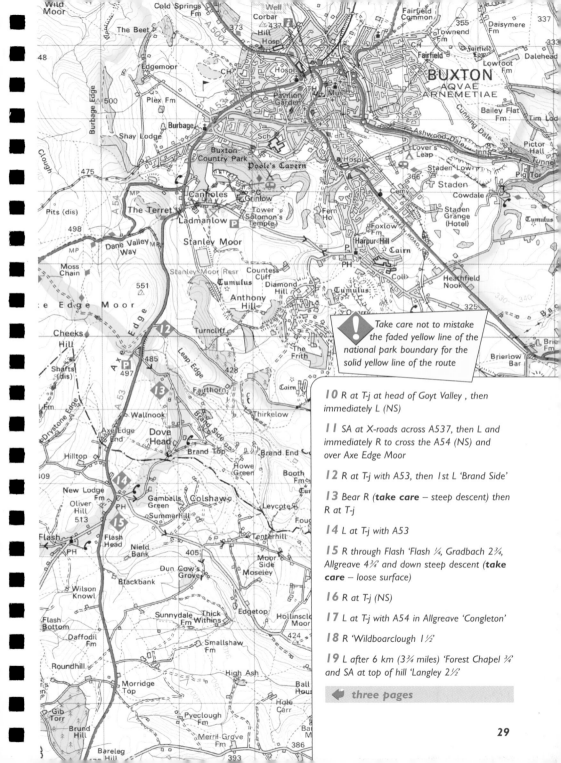

> **!** Take care not to mistake the faded yellow line of the national park boundary for the solid yellow line of the route

10 R at T-j at head of Goyt Valley , then immediately L (NS)

11 SA at X-roads across A537, then L and immediately R to cross the A54 (NS) and over Axe Edge Moor

12 R at T-j with A53, then 1st L 'Brand Side'

13 Bear R (**take care** – steep descent) then R at T-j

14 L at T-j with A53

15 R through Flash 'Flash ¼, Gradbach 2¾, Allgreave 4¾' and down steep descent (**take care** – loose surface)

16 R at T-j (NS)

17 L at T-j with A54 in Allgreave 'Congleton'

18 R 'Wildboarclough 1½'

19 L after 6 km (3¾ miles) 'Forest Chapel ¾' and SA at top of hill 'Langley 2½'

◀ **three pages**

29

5 *Winnats and Tideswell*

A ride of many contrasts, passing over the quieter millstone grit between New Mills and Mam Tor and again west of Dove Holes. The route crosses limestone country around the popular destinations of Castleton and Tideswell. There is a notable descent at Winnats Pass – a spectacular gorge and a favourite of mountain bikers.

Start

New Mills Central Station

P Several sites in New Mills

Distance and grade

54 km (34 miles)

Moderate/strenuous

Terrain

A mixture of the hilly and the more level upland plateau. Steep climbs from Wash, Bradwell, Tideswell and Monk's Dale, whereas Rushup Edge is easier. The descent into Combs is sharply bended and needs care. The off-road alternative at instruction 12 is slower and more demanding than the on-road equivalents

Refreshments

Plenty of choice in **New Mills**
Squirrels Inn, **Chinley**
Tea room at the Chestnut Centre
Plenty of choice in **Castleton**, **Bradwell** and **Tideswell**
Midland Hotel, **Peak Dale**
Beehive Hotel, **Combs**

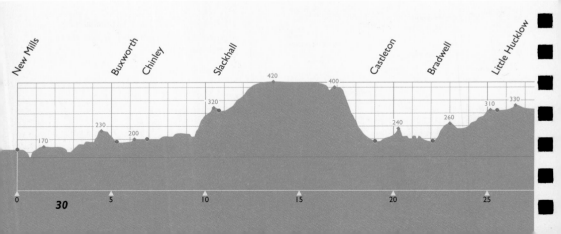

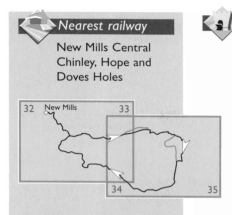

New Mills Central
Chinley, Hope and
Doves Holes

Places of interest

New Mills 1

A mill town, mostly 19th-century, once a centre of the calico printing trade. The former railway line between the town and Hayfield has been made into the Sett Valley Trail for walkers, cyclists and horse riders

Bradwell 13

A homely, former lead-mining village at the foot of Bradwell Dale. Hard miners' hats used to be made here. Bagshawe's Cavern, at the far end of an old lead mine and down 100 steps or so, is about 800 m (½ mile) long and contains remarkable rock formations.

▲ Winnats Pass

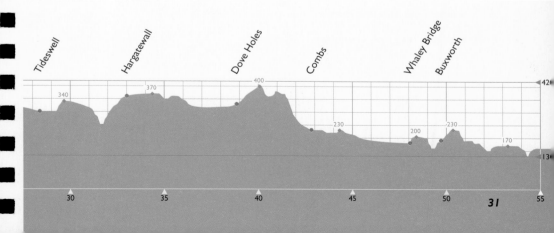

1 Leave New Mills Central Station and climb up station approach. R at T-j and R again Union Road

2 L at T-j Church Road 'Hayfield A6015'

3 3rd R Marsh Lane

4 L Ladypit Road, then bear R after going under bridge. Road becomes Dolly Lane

5 L at T-j, under railway bridge and through Chinley

6 1st L after junction with A624 'Wash 1/2' under railway bridge

7 Fork R and R again into Wash

8 L at T-j with A625 (**Or** for off-road route, go through gateway L in about 2 km (1¼ miles) – just after Rushup Lane on right – then R up sunken bridleway, over Lord's Seat, then bear L and sharp R at T-j with road and L at T-j with A625)

➡ **three pages**

19 L opposite Midland Hotel 'Batham Gate, Buxton' at T-j, across railway bridge and immediately R (NS)

20 SA at junction with A6 in Dove Holes 'Station', bear R over railway line, then L Cowlow Lane (NS). **Take care** – the descent to Combs is steep and twisting

21 Bear R past Beehive Hotel in Combs 'Chapel 2¾'

22 L at T-j 'Whaley Bridge B5470'

23 R in Horwich End just before light-controlled junction with A5004 Old Road with No Motor Vehicles sign

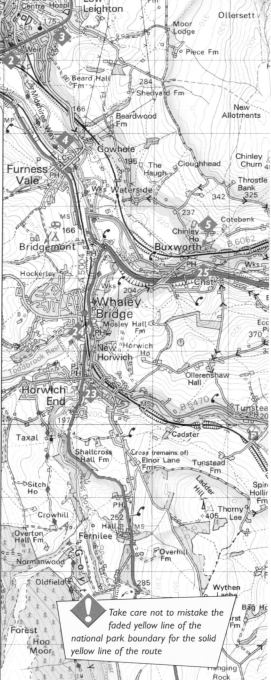

Take care not to mistake the faded yellow line of the national park boundary for the solid yellow line of the route

24 Easy to miss – 3rd R Bings Road, just before church on hill above road, then L at T-j (NS) in 1 km (¾ mile) to cross bridge over dual carriageway

25 R at T-j 'Chinley 1¼, Chapel 3½, Hayfield 5', under railway viaduct and immediately L Dolly Lane, returning to start

by reverse of outward route – R at T-j after going under low railway bridge in 3 km

(1¾ miles) 'New Mills 1¼', then L at X-roads, R Union Road at traffic lights, L at mini roundabout and 2nd L Station Road to return to start

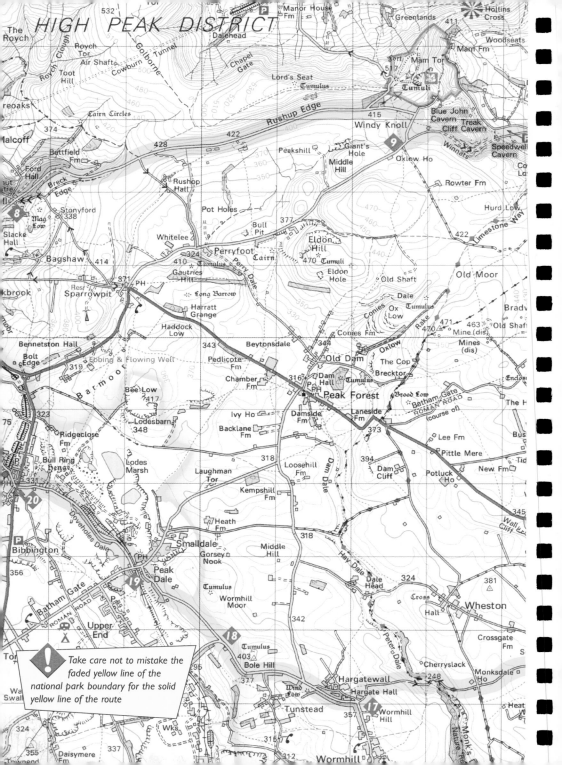

HIGH PEAK DISTRICT

Take care not to mistake the faded yellow line of the national park boundary for the solid yellow line of the route

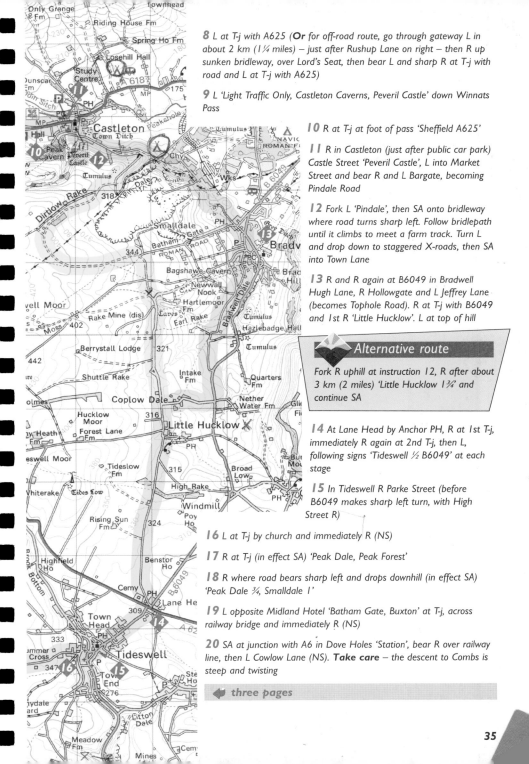

8 L at T-j with A625 (**Or** for off-road route, go through gateway L in about 2 km (1¼ miles) – just after Rushup Lane on right – then R up sunken bridleway, over Lord's Seat, then bear L and sharp R at T-j with road and L at T-j with A625)

9 L 'Light Traffic Only, Castleton Caverns, Peveril Castle' down Winnats Pass

10 R at T-j at foot of pass 'Sheffield A625'

11 R in Castleton (just after public car park) Castle Street 'Peveril Castle', L into Market Street and bear R and L Bargate, becoming Pindale Road

12 Fork L 'Pindale', then SA onto bridleway where road turns sharp left. Follow bridlepath until it climbs to meet a farm track. Turn L and drop down to staggered X-roads, then SA into Town Lane

13 R and R again at B6049 in Bradwell Hugh Lane, R Hollowgate and L Jeffrey Lane (becomes Tophole Road). R at T-j with B6049 and 1st R 'Little Hucklow'. L at top of hill

Alternative route

Fork R uphill at instruction 12, R after about 3 km (2 miles) 'Little Hucklow 1¾ and continue SA

14 At Lane Head by Anchor PH, R at 1st T-j, immediately R again at 2nd T-j, then L, following signs 'Tideswell ½ B6049' at each stage

15 In Tideswell R Parke Street (before B6049 makes sharp left turn, with High Street R)

16 L at T-j by church and immediately R (NS)

17 R at T-j (in effect SA) 'Peak Dale, Peak Forest'

18 R where road bears sharp left and drops downhill (in effect SA) 'Peak Dale ¾, Smalldale 1'

19 L opposite Midland Hotel 'Batham Gate, Buxton' at T-j, across railway bridge and immediately R (NS)

20 SA at junction with A6 in Dove Holes 'Station', bear R over railway line, then L Cowlow Lane (NS). **Take care** – the descent to Combs is steep and twisting

three pages

6 *Last of the Summer Wine*

A tour of the magnificent countryside between Barnsley and Holmfirth. Though it only touches on the National Park, and passes through parts of the lowland West Riding, it is mostly in the Pennine millstone grit country. An alternative part of the Trans-Pennine Cycle Route is due to run along the former railway line between Dunford Bridge and Penistone and will give an easier return to Penistone when it is opened.

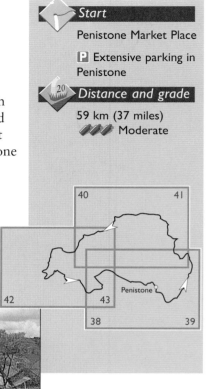

Start

Penistone Market Place

P Extensive parking in Penistone

Distance and grade

59 km (37 miles)

Moderate

The Holme Valley

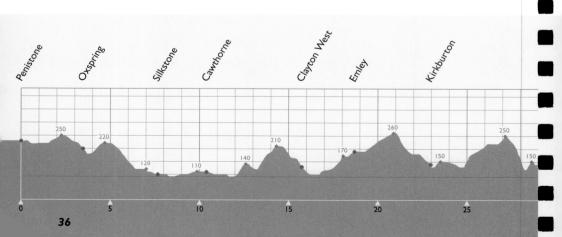

Terrain
The countryside is almost entirely upland. Several steep-walled valleys to be crossed and long sections along hilltops. Some off-road cycling round the head of the Holme Valley

Nearest railway
Penistone and Stockwood

Places of interest

Cawthorne *10*
A village with a late 19th-century church and a delightful local museum. To its west lies Cannon Hall Country Park and Museum. The house and grounds date from the 18th-century. There is also a regimental museum that includes a model display of the Charge of the Light Brigade, Victorian kitchens (open in the summer) and a Visitor Centre with exhibits relating to the house, gardens and village

Holmfirth *24*
Now, fittingly, the home of BBC TV's *Last of the Summer Wine*, it was the home of the comic picture post-card in the late 19th-century and the company's proprietor, James Bamforth, tried to establish an English film industry here in the early years of this century.

Refreshments

Plenty of choice in **Penistone**
Spencer Arms, **Cawthorne**
Cafes at Cannon Hall Country Park (Sundays) and Garden Centre (opposite main car park)
Pubs in **Emley** *and* **Kirkburton**
Plenty of choice in **Holmfirth**
Pubs in **Upperthong**
Pubs in **Dunford Bridge** *and* **Victoria**

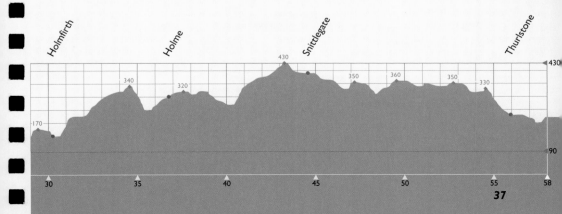

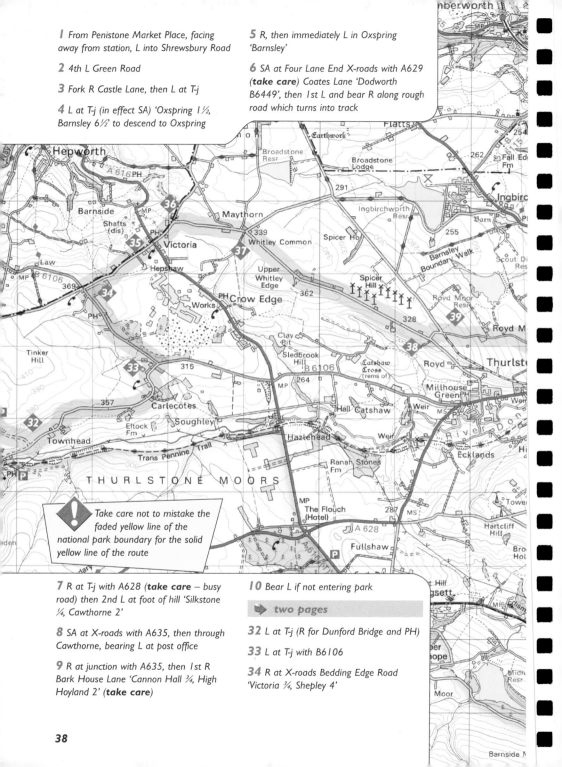

1 From Penistone Market Place, facing away from station, L into Shrewsbury Road

2 4th L Green Road

3 Fork R Castle Lane, then L at T-j

4 L at T-j (in effect SA) 'Oxspring 1½, Barnsley 6½' to descend to Oxspring

5 R, then immediately L in Oxspring 'Barnsley'

6 SA at Four Lane End X-roads with A629 (**take care**) Coates Lane 'Dodworth B6449', then 1st L and bear R along rough road which turns into track

Take care not to mistake the faded yellow line of the national park boundary for the solid yellow line of the route

7 R at T-j with A628 (**take care** – busy road) then 2nd L at foot of hill 'Silkstone ¼, Cawthorne 2'

8 SA at X-roads with A635, then through Cawthorne, bearing L at post office

9 R at junction with A635, then 1st R Bark House Lane 'Cannon Hall ¾, High Hoyland 2' (**take care**)

10 Bear L if not entering park

➡️ **two pages**

32 L at T-j (R for Dunford Bridge and PH)

33 L at T-j with B6106

34 R at X-roads Bedding Edge Road 'Victoria ¾, Shepley 4'

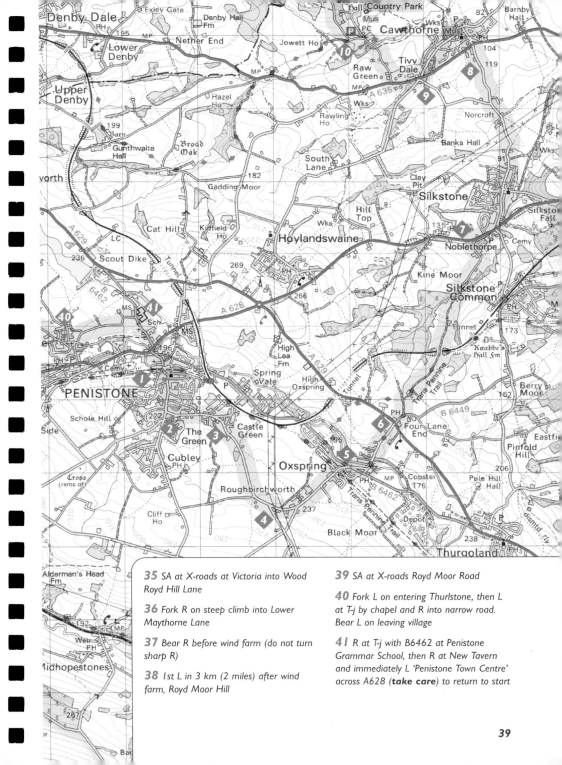

35 SA at X-roads at Victoria into Wood Royd Hill Lane

36 Fork R on steep climb into Lower Maythorne Lane

37 Bear R before wind farm (do not turn sharp R)

38 1st L in 3 km (2 miles) after wind farm, Royd Moor Hill

39 SA at X-roads Royd Moor Road

40 Fork L on entering Thurlstone, then L at T-j by chapel and R into narrow road. Bear L on leaving village

41 R at T-j with B6462 at Penistone Grammar School, then R at New Tavern and immediately L 'Penistone Town Centre' across A628 (**take care**) to return to start

9 R at junction with A635, then 1st R Bark House Lane 'Cannon Hall ¾, High Hoyland 2' (**take care**)

10 Bear L if not entering park

11 Sharp L back on yourself on entering High Hoyland 'Clayton West 1¼'

12 R at T-j with A636 at far end of Clayton West (**take care** – fast cars) then 3rd L in 400 m (yd) Kiln Lane 'Emley 1½'

13 L at T-j approaching Emley 'Emley ½'

14 Fork R at base of TV mast 'Jagger Lane'

15 Road bears L

16 R B6116 and immediately L in Kirkburton

17 Cross A629 (**take care**) at oblique X-roads 'Stocksmoor 1, Thurstonland 2, New Mill 3'

18 R Stocksmoor Road 'Stocksmoor' by PH

19 Road bears L

20 SA across A616 Luke Lane, then bear L

21 R at T-j

22 4th L onto bridleway Berry Back Lane and take lower track at fork

23 Very obliquely R onto A635 (**take care**)

➡ *two pages*

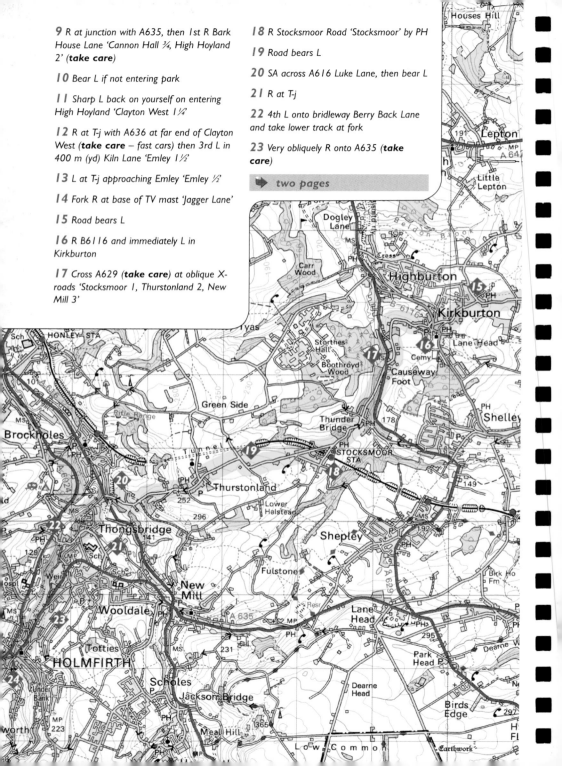

18 R Stocksmoor Road 'Stocksmoor' by PH

19 Road bears L

20 SA across A616 Luke Lane, then bear L

21 R at T-j

22 4th L onto bridleway Berry Back Lane and take lower track at fork

23 Very obliquely R onto A635 (**take care**)

24 In centre of Holmfirth bear R at junction with B6106 Victoria Street, then L at T-j with A6024 and fork 1st R Upperthong Lane

25 L by PH Broad Lane and L again Dean Road

26 L at T-j by Ford Inn 'Holmfirth, Greenfield', then SA at X-roads Green Gate Lane

27 R at T-j with A6024 in Holme

28 L onto sandy forest track, contour round, then across Yateholme Dam and rise

29 Where track bears L at house, take track R 'public bridleway' onto Kirklees Way and follow uphill

30 Hard R at 5-way junction of minor routes at end of track

31 R towards Dunford Bridge by 'Welcome to Barnsley' sign

32 L at T-j (R for Dunford Bridge and PH)

33 L at T-j with B6106

34 R at X-roads Bedding Edge Road 'Victoria ¾, Shepley 4'

35 SA at X-roads at Victoria into Wood Royd Hill Lane

36 Fork R on steep climb into Lower Maythorne Lane

37 Bear R before wind farm (do not turn sharp R)

 four pages

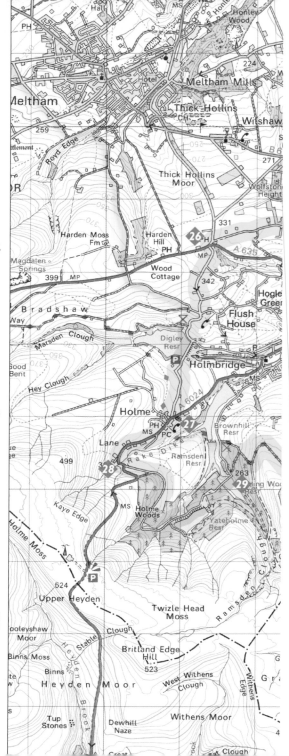

Take care not to mistake the faded yellow line of the national park boundary for the solid yellow line of the route

Loxley Valley

A ride around the moors and reservoirs west of the built-up area but almost entirely within the boundaries of the metropolitan district of Sheffield. Through the villages of High and Low Bradfield and the hamlet of Strines. High-level sections offer good views across the River Don to Wharncliffe and along the Loxley Valley.

Start

Junction of Myers Grove Lane with Wood Lane at the Malinbridge end

P There are several public off-street car parks in the city, but none close to the start of the ride. People using nearby pubs may be able to use their car parks – please ask

▶ *Bradfield Dale from High Bradfield*

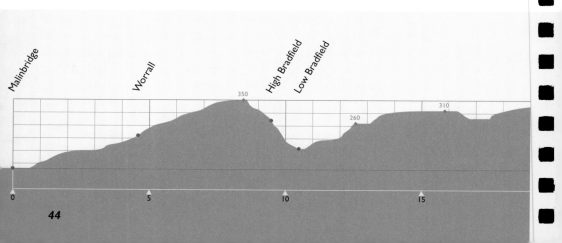

38 km (24 miles)

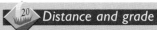 Moderate/ strenuous

 Terrain

Several climbs up the steep sides of Loxley Valley, but there are long upland sections between Worrall and High Bradfield and from Strines to Ughill. The return to Malinbridge follows an old track

Nearest railway

Sheffield

 Places of interest

Strines 8/9
The Inn was once a small manor house. Across the valley is Boot's Folly, built for a Sheffield contractor who lived nearby to keep his workforce occupied

Loxley Valley 15
A valley of reservoirs, formerly a centre of the metal industry when the river powered numerous small workshops. The dam above Bradfield (Dale Dyke) broke in 1865 resulting in the deaths of some 240 people and the destruction of about 600 buildings downstream

 Refreshments

Old Horns Inn, **High Bradfield**
Strines Inn, **Strines**
PH in **Dungworth** (SA instead of L at instruction 13)
Pubs in and around **Malinbridge**

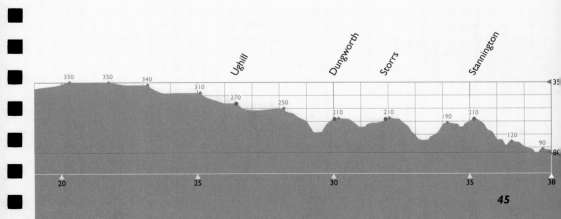

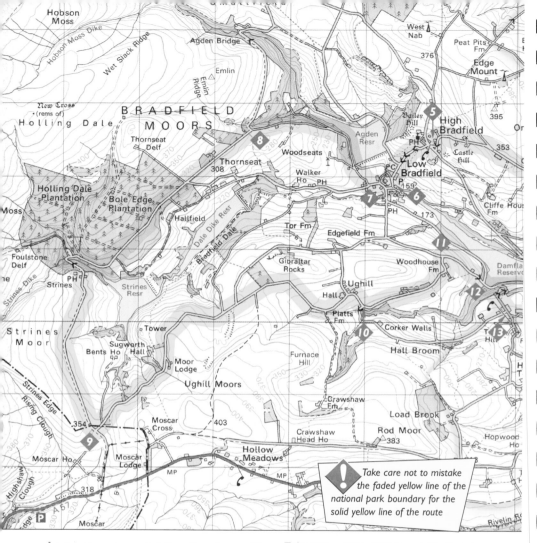

Take care not to mistake the faded yellow line of the national park boundary for the solid yellow line of the route

1 L from the eastern end of Myers Grove Lane and L into Stannington Road

2 Bear L into Loxley Road, just after crossing river, fork R into Wisewood Lane (becoming Hallowmoor Road) and SA at X-roads into Rural Lane

3 Obliquely L at T-j (NS)

4 L Kirk Edge Road at triangular junction entering Worrall 'High Bradfield 3, Loxley 1¼'

5 Bear L Little Lane 'Loxley 3, Sheffield 7', then R at T-j and L Woodfall Lane 'Low Bradfield ½, Dungworth 2½'.

Take care – steep gradients and risk of missing junctions

6 L The Sands at 1st T-j in Low Bradfield, then sharp R Smithy Bridge Road 'Dungworth 1½, Sheffield 7', across River Loxley and R at 2nd T-j Fairhouse Lane 'Penistone 10, Strines'

7 1st R Windy Bank 'Midhopestones 7, Penistone 10'

8 L at T-j (NS)

9 L just after cattle grid about 2 km (1¼ miles) after passing through Strines hamlet 'Ughill 3, Dunghill 5'

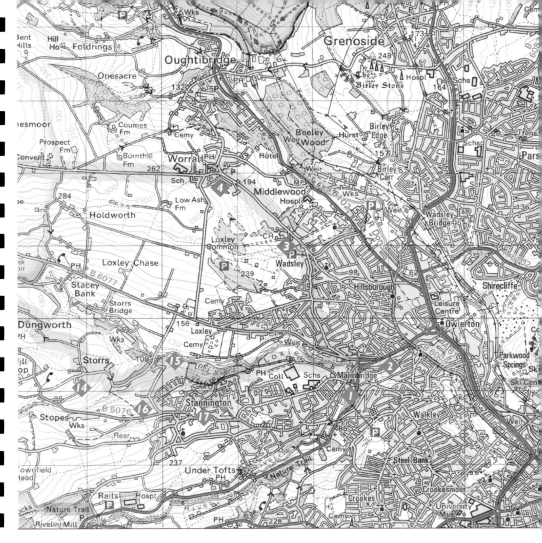

10 4th L in about 5½ km (3½ miles) Ughill Wood Lane 'Bradfield 2'

11 R at T-j 'Dungworth 1¼'

12 R at T-j (in effect SA) 'Dungworth ¾, Sheffield 6', then R uphill 'Dungworth ½, Stannington 2½'

13 1st L Dungworth Green 'Storrs 1', passing school R

14 Bear L in Storrs 'Loxley 1¼. **Take care** descending steep, twisting lane

15 R 'Stannington ½, Sheffield 5'

16 L Acorn Way (NS) and bear L at bus turning place into Acorn Drive

17 L at T-j (Greaves Lane sign further down road) going SA past 'Public Byway' sign downhill. The surface deteriorates once the last house is passed on the right. In about 500 m (yd) come to Robin Hood PH on left, and join its access drive, then L at T-j into Myers Grove Lane to return to start

Burbage, Eyam and Froggatt

This ride mixes the shade of Ecclesall Woods, the high moorland southwest of Sheffield, the edges on the east of the Derwent Valley. Linking the little town of Hathersage, the Barrell Road through Bretton and the villages of Great Hucklow, Foolow and Eyam, which were once busy with mining and quarrying. It can be started at several points *en route* but for convenience, the instructions start at Dore Station.

Start

Dore Station

P There is some on-road parking in Abbeydale Road, Dore, beside Ecclesall Woods Public parking at Ringinglow and at Upper Burbage bridge

Distance and grade

50 km (31 miles)
Moderate

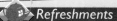
Refreshments

Cafe at **Abbeydale** Industrial Hamlet
Norfolk Arms PH, **Ringinglow**
Plenty of choice in **Hathersage** and **Eyam**
Barrell Inn, **Bretton**
Queen Anne PH, **Great Hucklow**
Lazy Landlord PH, **Foolow**
Several pubs between **Froggatt** and **Bradway**

▶ *Rilley Graves at Eyam*

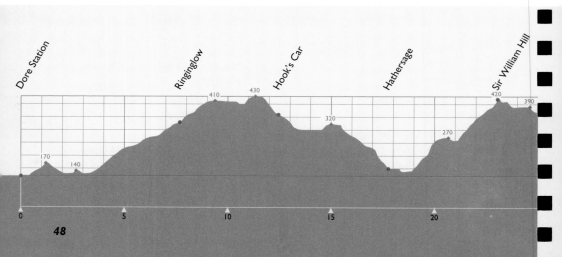

Three main climbs: from Dore up to Burbage Rocks, from Leadmill Bridge to Sir William Hill and out of the Derwent Valley over Froggatt Edge. They mostly call for stamina rather than great effort, though there are some sharp pitches on the climb from Hathersage to Sir William Hill

Nearest railway

Sheffield, Dore, Hathersage and Grindleford

Hathersage 10

Hathersage was an industrial town until this century, with various metalwork trades linked with wire-drawing: nailmaking, pinmaking and needles. The leading family was once that of Eyre. Charlotte Bronte used the name and other local elements in 'Jane Eyre', where the town is called 'Morton', and her 'Thornfield Hall' may be modelled on North Lees Hall

Eyam 17

Once a mining and still a quarrying centre. Eyam's chief historical association is with the outbreak of Plague, which, it is supposed, arrived in a bolt of cloth from London in 1665. William Mompesson, the Rector, with his predecessor Thomas Stanley (who had been ejected under the Act of Conformity in 1662) organized a quarantine of the villagers, over 80% of whom died. There is a museum facing the car park in the former Methodist church at the west end of the village

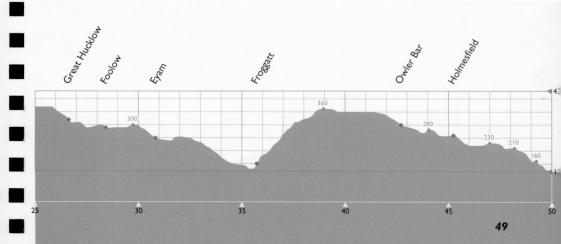

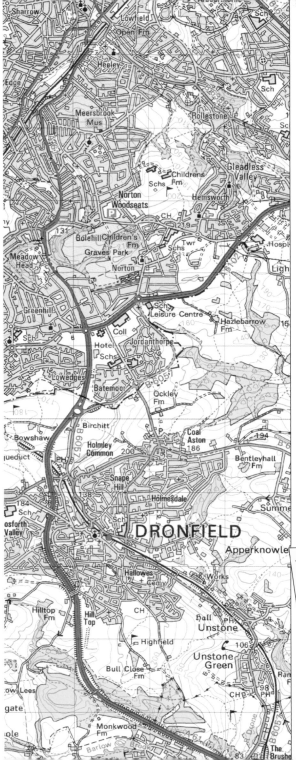

1 R at the exit from Dore Station into Abbeydale Road

2 L into Ecclesall Wood 'Public Bridleway' (opposite Beauchief Gardens). From sign 'Public Bridleway to Dore' take next track R and continue SA, bearing gently R and climbing. After about 800 m (½ mile) track turns further R ('Horse Riding Prohibited' on left) and begin to drop down, passing between two 'Public Footpath' signs

3 Track leads to Abbey Lane where R and then L onto further bridleway, just before Abbey Croft cul-de-sac. **Take care** – busy road. Fork L in woods where a signed public footpath crosses the route

4 R onto Whirlowdale Road which crosses track

5 L Whirlowdale Crescent and ascend to T-j along Millhouses Lane, where L, then bear R into Silverdale Road at upper end

6 SA at X-roads into Knowle Lane and SA (becomes Ringinglow Road)

➡ next page

21 At Owler Bar (one-way – **take care**) pass Peacock Inn and take turning 'Holmesfield, Dronfield B6054' by Moorlands Inn. SA through Holmesfield, Dronfield Woodhouse and Mickley, following signs for B6054

22 R at T-j in Upper Bradway 'Sheffield (A61)', then L 'Dore 2, Millhouses 2¼' and down Twentywell Lane to T-j with A621 where R 'Sheffield A621' and immediately R again to return to Dore Station

⚠ Take care not to mistake the faded yellow line of the national park boundary for the solid yellow line of the route

7 Fork R 'Ladybower 6' after Burbage Rocks car park and just before cattle grid

8 R 'Ladybower 5'

9 R 'Ladybower 4'

10 L into Jagger's Lane, then L at T-j and R onto B6001 'Grindleford 3, Baslow 5' in Hathersage

11 R at brow of hill just after Plough PH

12 R at T-j (NS)

13 R (in effect SA) onto track over Sir William Hill where sealed road bears sharp L. R (in effect SA) at end of track, following Barrell Road along ridge (**Or** sharp L for short cut to Eyam, then L again at T-j just after Eyam Museum on right to join main route at instruction 17)

14 L at entrance to Great Hucklow 'Grindlow ¼'. SA through Grindlow

15 L at T-j (NS)

16 SA in Foolow, following signs for 'Eyam' or 'Eyam, Grindleford'

17 L at T-j entering Square in Eyam 'Hathersage B6521'

18 **Take care** – R at T-j with B6001 'Bakewell B6001'. L 'Froggatt' and descend steeply to bridge across River Derwent, then L Hallowgate and R uphill at Rose Cottage

19 L at T-j 'Calver B6054 1½' and up across face of Froggatt Edge through woods

20 R at T-j 'Dronfield B6054, Owler Bar 2'

◀ *previous page*

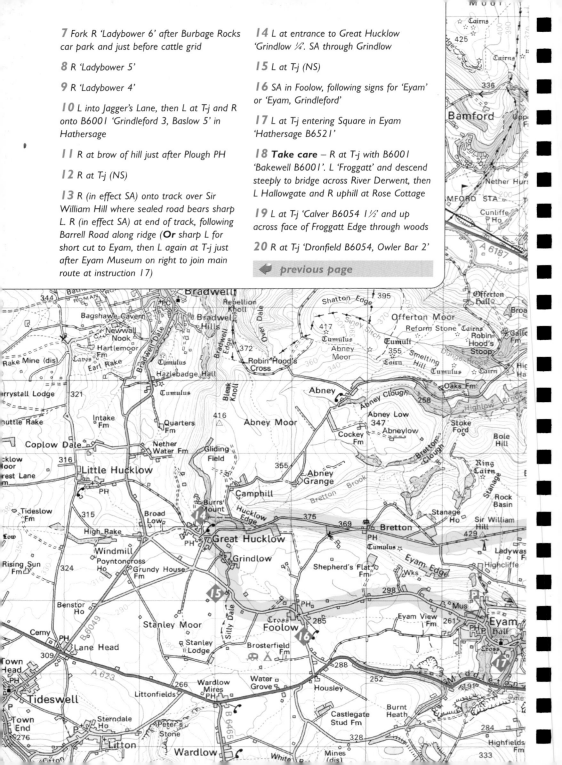

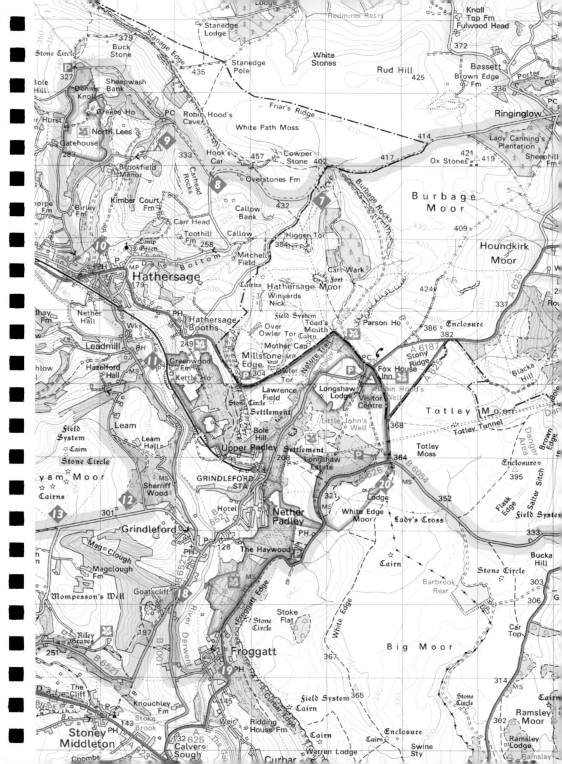

Between Chesterfield and Bakewell

A ride with much to offer. There are several off-road sections on a variety of surfaces between Calver and Hell Bank and excellent views on the climb from Common Side to Bole Hill, over High Rake and as you leave Bakewell. Between Longstone and Bakewell, the ride follows the Monsal Trail. This is a section of the old Midland Railway's main line between London and Manchester that closed down in the 1960s and has been converted into a route for non-motor traffic.

Start

Chesterfield Tourist Information Centre

P Several long-stay car parks in Chesterfield

Distance and grade

48 km (30 miles)

🚴🚴🚴🚴 Moderate/strenuous

Terrain

A route set mostly against the lie of the land with lengthy climbs from Common Side and from Beeley Lodge and sharp ascents from Calver (off-road) and Bakewell. The descents into the Derwent Valley (over Curbar Edge and into Edensor) need some care

Refreshments

Plenty of choice in **Chesterfield**
Tea shop in **Barlow**
Tea shop and PH at **Calver Bridge**
Eyre Arms, **Hassop**
The Crispin PH, **Great Longstone**
Plenty of choice in **Bakewell**
Tea shop in **Edensor**
Cafe at Calton Lees garden centre
Devonshire Arms, **Beeley**

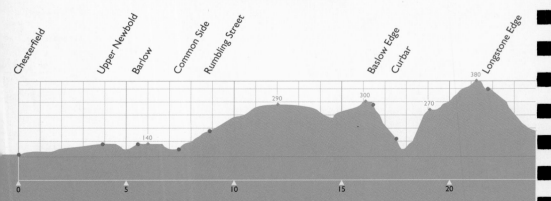

56 57

58 59

Chesterfield

Places of interest

Chesterfield 1

The core of the town is the mostly traffic-free Market Place, which deserves some time to visit. The crooked spire of the parish church catches the eye, but the rest of the church is of interest. Much dates from the 14th and 15th-centuries and there are side chapels that reflect the medieval wealth of the town

Edensor 17

A village on the Chatsworth estate (pronounced 'Enser') planned by Joseph Paxton (the Duke's head gardener) and aided in the design of the houses by John Robertson of Derby. The village displays a range of Victorian villa architecture. Buildings date from 1839 to around 1850 and were probably an attempt to create an 'improved' model village some time after the old settlement had been removed

◀ Edensor

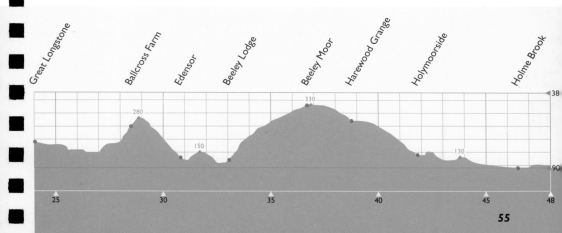

Great Longstone · Ballcross Farm · Edensor · Beeley Lodge · Beeley Moor · Harewood Grange · Holymoorside · Holme Brook

280 · 150 · 330 · 130 · 38 · 90

25 · 30 · 35 · 40 · 45 · 48

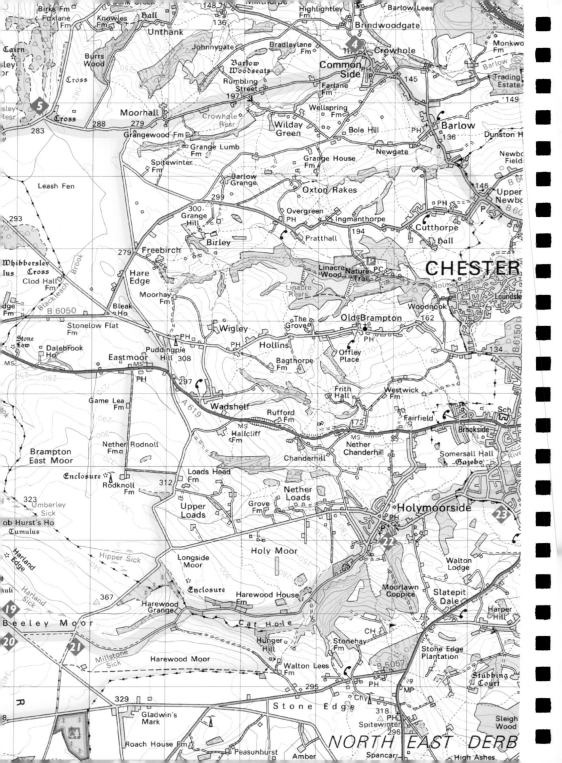

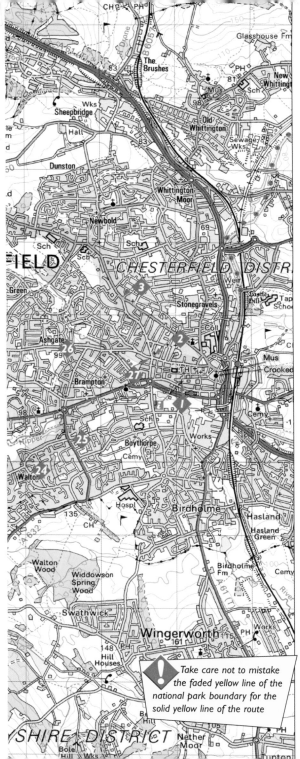

1 From Chesterfield Tourist Information Centre cross Market Place with Market Hall on your right, then up Soresby Street and SA at X-roads with Rose Hill. L at T-j with Saltersgate

2 R where Saltersgate becomes Ashgate Road, into Compton Street, bear L into West Street, then along Hawksley Avenue

3 L at T-j with main road (B6051, NS). SA for about 6½ km (4 miles) through Upper Newbold, Barlow and Common Side

4 L at triangular junction just before delimitation sign at end of Common Side and uphill for 3 km (2 miles) Farley Lane (NS). SA to enter Peak National Park near top of climb

5 L at T-j 'Baslow 4'

➡ next page

20 L after 800 m (½ mile) on Beeley Moor where open triangular green begins (NS)

21 SA at X-roads after 600 m (yd) (NS)

22 R at X-roads by Bull's Head PH in Holymoorside

23 L in 2 km (1¼ mile) Park Hall Avenue, L again at T-j Somersby Avenue (becomes Breckland Road)

24 L at T-j Moorland View Road and bear R

25 L at further T-j after 800 m (½ mile) and descend to mini-roundabout where SA, then SA again at X-roads with traffic lights and at further X-roads in 100 m (yd) into Old Hall Road

26 R at T-j

27 SA at X-road with traffic lights and R into one-way street Clarence Road and downhill to T-j with traffic lights where L, then bear L into West Bars and dismount at 'No Entry' signs. The Tourist Information Centre is on your right a further 100 m (yd) along Low Pavement

Take care not to mistake the faded yellow line of the national park boundary for the solid yellow line of the route

6 L at T-j with A621 'Baslow 1½', then R at staggered X-roads 'Curbar 2'. R after car park and descend Curbar Edge. **Take care** – steep descent

7 R at T-j opposite Bridge Inn and R at T-j onto A623 'Stockport, Manchester A623'

8 1st L 'Calver village' bearing L where Main Street becomes High Street

9 L at T-j with B6001 'Bakewell', then shortly after T-j go through field gate on your right and follow track across hillside

10 Bear R where track comes in obliquely on your left

11 Bear R onto unsealed road along ridge of Longstone Edge. **Take care** – quarry traffic. Pass over High Rake and descend to cattle grid

12 Through metal gate and L onto road, then bear R down Longstone Edge, bearing L near foot

13 L at T-j entering Great Longstone 'Rowland, Hassop, Ashford' (in effect SA) through village and bear R

14 Sharp L in 400 m (¼ mile) just before bridge over road, then immediately R at end of fence onto access path to 'Monsal Trail', turning away from bridge along Trail towards Bakewell (information notice by path entrance). Continue along Monsal Trail for about 3 km (2 miles)

15 At Bakewell Station take path on R alongside side of station buildings nearest to you into car park. Turn L at car park exit and L again 'Unsuitable for Lorries' over bridge across former railway line. Pass golf course and after about 800 m (½ mile) road turns R back on itself steeply uphill

16 After about 2 km (1¼ miles) take rough track forking R by sycamore tree. **Take care** – poor surface. After a further 2 km (1¼ miles), road surface becomes sealed and enters Edensor village

17 Keep village green on your R cross cattle grid. R onto B6012 and after 2 km (1¼ miles) cross bridge

18 Bear L where sign shows No through road, and climb along clearly defined track once tarmac ends

19 L at junction with surfaced road

Take care not to mistake the faded yellow line of the national park boundary for the solid yellow line of the route

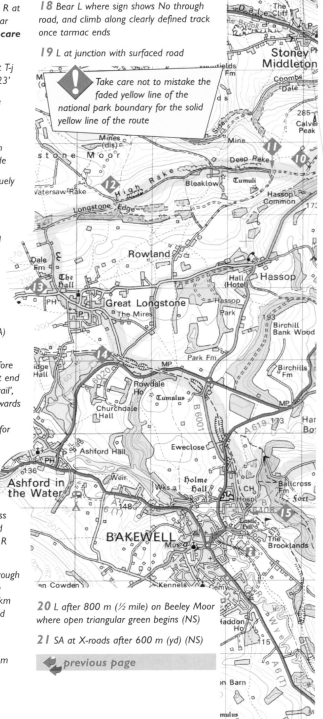

20 L after 800 m (½ mile) on Beeley Moor where open triangular green begins (NS)

21 SA at X-roads after 600 m (yd) (NS)

previous page

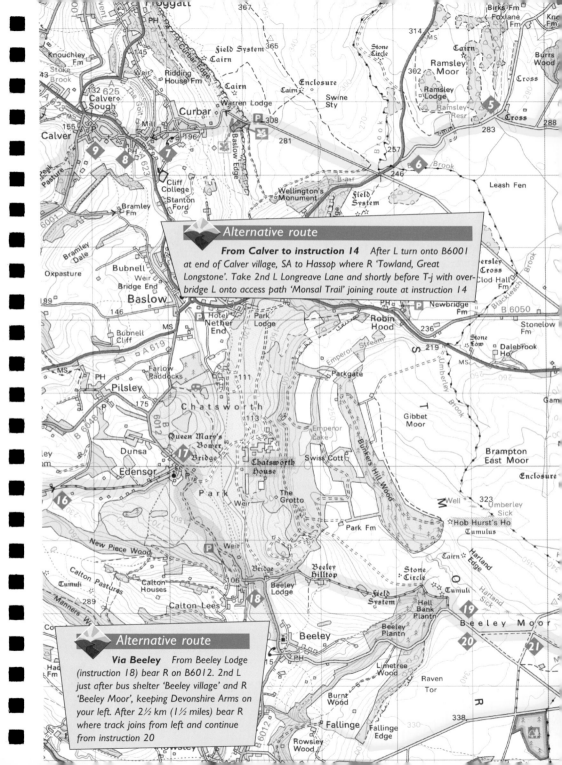

Alternative route

From Calver to instruction 14 After L turn onto B6001 at end of Calver village, SA to Hassop where R 'Towland, Great Longstone'. Take 2nd L Longreave Lane and shortly before T-j with over-bridge L onto access path 'Monsal Trail' joining route at instruction 14

Alternative route

Via Beeley From Beeley Lodge (instruction 18) bear R on B6012. 2nd L just after bus shelter 'Beeley village' and R 'Beeley Moor', keeping Devonshire Arms on your left. After 2½ km (1½ miles) bear R where track joins from left and continue from instruction 20

From Cromford, visiting industrial sites and quiet countryside

A short ride with plenty of interest and plenty of contrast. There is much industrial archaeology in the early part of the ride but later it becomes much more rural. The waterside at Ogston Reservoir or the picturesque village of Ashover offer excellent spots for a picnic.

▶ Cromford

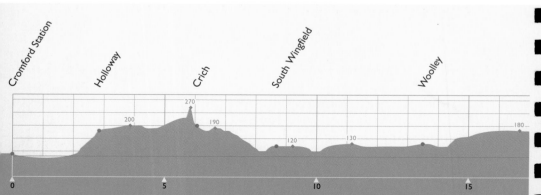

South Wingfield 4

The romantic ruins of medieval Wingfield Manor are notable. One of Mary Queen of Scots' many places of incarceration in or near the Peak, it was damaged during the English Civil War and much of its masonry reused in the 18th-century. The village church, off-route down Church Lane, is mainly 13th-century. The buildings of the former railway station of 1840 nearby are also worth seeing, the last surviving of Francis Thompson's classical work for the North Midland Railway

Matlock 19–21

A collection of villages that grew as a 19th-century spa, once the road through Scarthin Nick (now the A6) was opened in 1818, and the railway from Ambergate in 1849, under the aegis of the Smedley family, whose Riber Castle high above the town dominates many views. The hydropathic hotel John Smedley had built in 1853 is now the headquarters of the County Council. Tourism is now chiefly at Matlock Bath, with the diversions of attractions such as Gulliver's World, the Heights of Abraham, attainable by a funicular, and the Peak District Mining Museum.

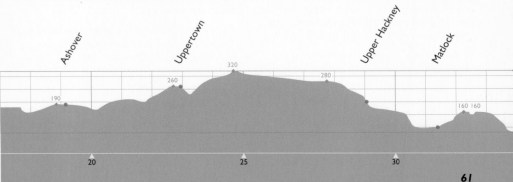

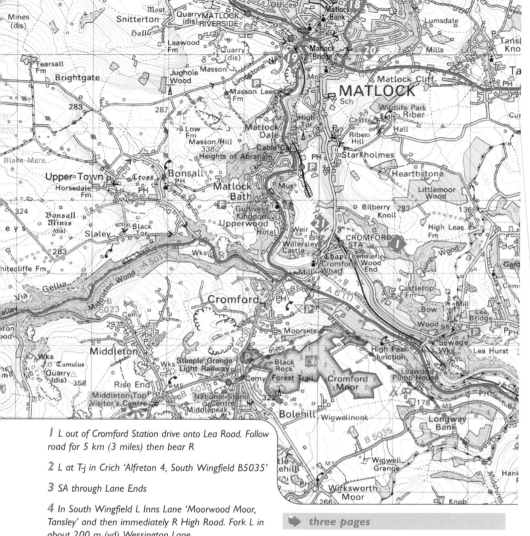

1 L out of Cromford Station drive onto Lea Road. Follow road for 5 km (3 miles) then bear R

2 L at T-j in Crich 'Alfreton 4, South Wingfield B5035'

3 SA through Lane Ends

4 In South Wingfield L Inns Lane 'Moorwood Moor, Tansley' and then immediately R High Road. Fork L in about 200 m (yd) Wessington Lane

5 L 'Matlock 5¾ A615' at T-j with A615, then R Cross Lane 'Higham' on entering Wessington where main road bears L – **take care**. R at T-j (NS)

6 **Easy to miss** – L after about 150 m (yd) 'Brackenfield' bearing sharp R 'Brackenfield' in 800 m (½ mile)

7 R at T-j by church 'Woolley Moor 1¾'

8 R at T-j 'Clay Cross, Tibshelf B6014', then 1st L just after crossing small arm of reservoir 'Woolley Moor'. Bear L in village

➡️ *three pages*

18 In Matlock Bank R at X-roads Bank Street. **Take care** – very steep in parts

19 In Matlock Bridge L at roundabout Causeway Road (becomes Causeway Lane, then Matlock Green) 'Motorway M1, A615 Chesterfield (A632)'

20 In Matlock Green R at X-roads Church Street (becomes Starkholmes Road, then Willersley Road/Lane) 'Starkholmes'

21 L almost back on yourself at T-j Lea Road 'Lea, Holloway, Crich' and L again up Cromford Station approach

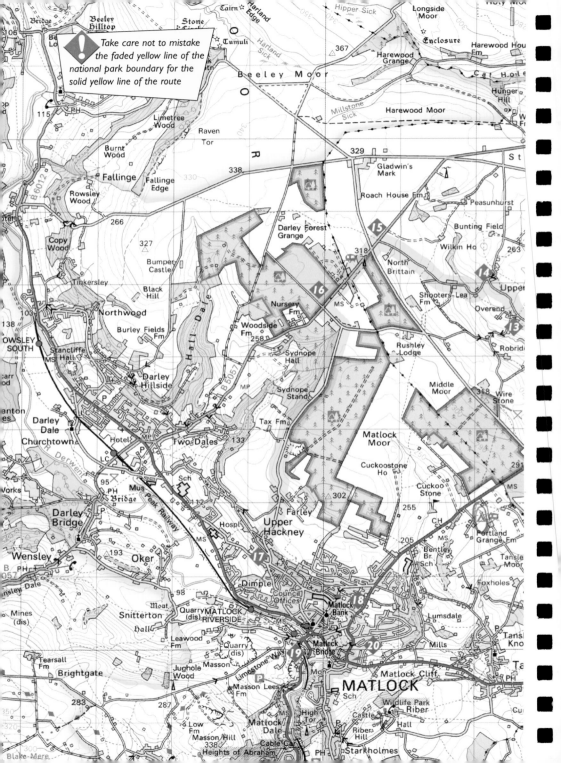

Take care not to mistake the faded yellow line of the national park boundary for the solid yellow line of the route

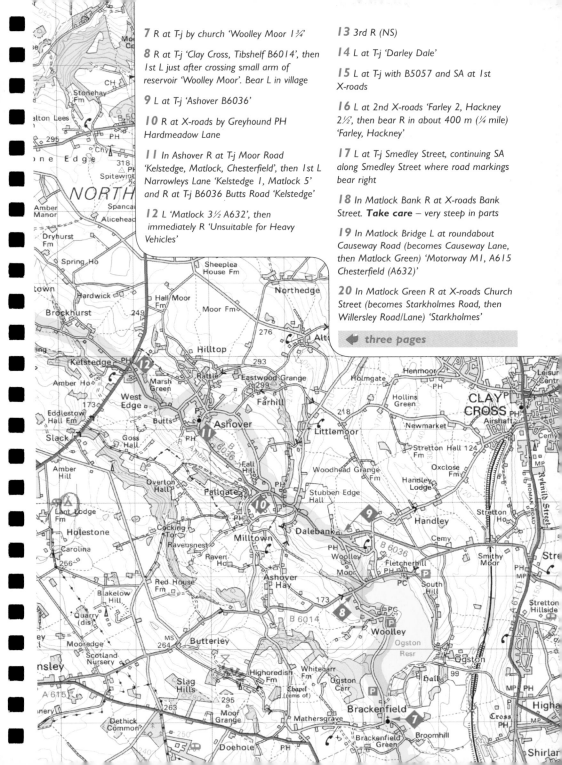

7 R at T-j by church 'Woolley Moor 1¾'

8 R at T-j 'Clay Cross, Tibshelf B6014', then 1st L just after crossing small arm of reservoir 'Woolley Moor'. Bear L in village

9 L at T-j 'Ashover B6036'

10 R at X-roads by Greyhound PH Hardmeadow Lane

11 In Ashover R at T-j Moor Road 'Kelstedge, Matlock, Chesterfield', then 1st L Narrowleys Lane 'Kelstedge 1, Matlock 5' and R at T-j B6036 Butts Road 'Kelstedge'

12 L 'Matlock 3½ A632', then immediately R 'Unsuitable for Heavy Vehicles'

13 3rd R (NS)

14 L at T-j 'Darley Dale'

15 L at T-j with B5057 and SA at 1st X-roads

16 L at 2nd X-roads 'Farley 2, Hackney 2½', then bear R in about 400 m (¼ mile) 'Farley, Hackney'

17 L at T-j Smedley Street, continuing SA along Smedley Street where road markings bear right

18 In Matlock Bank R at X-roads Bank Street. **Take care** – very steep in parts

19 In Matlock Bridge L at roundabout Causeway Road (becomes Causeway Lane, then Matlock Green) 'Motorway M1, A615 Chesterfield (A632)'

20 In Matlock Green R at X-roads Church Street (becomes Starkholmes Road, then Willersley Road/Lane) 'Starkholmes'

◀ three pages

Two Trails and the Barmote

A ride along two of the old railway lines converted into trails for walkers, riders and cyclists. The trails can be busy on fine summer weekends and Bank holidays.

▲ *The High Peak Trail near Minninglow Hill*

Start

Cromford Station or Wirksworth or the cycle hire centres at Middleton Top and Parsley Hay

P Cromford Station and Middleton Top Visitor Centre

Distance and grade

59 km (37 miles)
Easy

Terrain

The High Peak and Tissinton Trails offer easy cycling, although there are two steep inclines near the Cromford start. There are climbs from the turning for Bradbourne and past Brassington on the return leg

Nearest railway

Cromford

Refreshments

Drinks and snacks at **Cromford Wharf, Middleton Top** *and* **Parsley Hay**
Teas at **Gotham Grange** *and* **Tissington**
Pubs in **Brassington**
Plenty of choice in **Wirksworth**

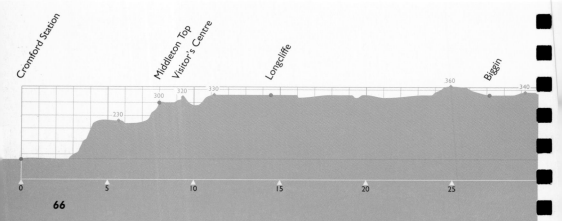

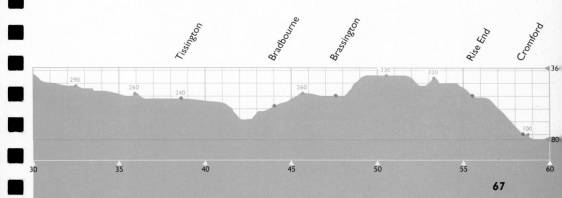

Places of interest

Tissington Trail *8/9*
This popular long-distance path for walkers, horse riders and cyclists follows the route of the old London and North Western Railway's link from the Cromford and High Peak line to Ashbourne. Stretches of the cutting are nature reserves

▲ *Tissington*

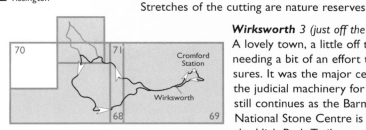

Wirksworth *3 (just off the route)*
A lovely town, a little off the beaten track, needing a bit of an effort to find some of its treasures. It was the major centre of lead mining and the judicial machinery for regulating the industry still continues as the Barmote Court. The National Stone Centre is to the north-west, near the High Peak Trail

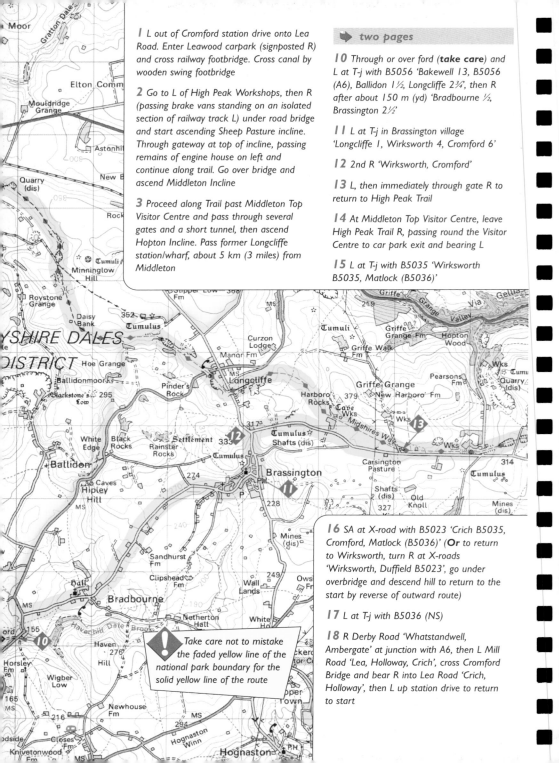

1 L out of Cromford station drive onto Lea Road. Enter Leawood carpark (signposted R) and cross railway footbridge. Cross canal by wooden swing footbridge

2 Go to L of High Peak Workshops, then R (passing brake vans standing on an isolated section of railway track L) under road bridge and start ascending Sheep Pasture incline. Through gateway at top of incline, passing remains of engine house on left and continue along trail. Go over bridge and ascend Middleton Incline

3 Proceed along Trail past Middleton Top Visitor Centre and pass through several gates and a short tunnel, then ascend Hopton Incline. Pass former Longcliffe station/wharf, about 5 km (3 miles) from Middleton

➡ *two pages*

10 Through or over ford (**take care**) and L at T-j with B5056 'Bakewell 13, B5056 (A6), Ballidon 1½, Longcliffe 2¾', then R after about 150 m (yd) 'Bradbourne ½, Brassington 2½'

11 L at T-j in Brassington village 'Longcliffe 1, Wirksworth 4, Cromford 6'

12 2nd R 'Wirksworth, Cromford'

13 L, then immediately through gate R to return to High Peak Trail

14 At Middleton Top Visitor Centre, leave High Peak Trail R, passing round the Visitor Centre to car park exit and bearing L

15 L at T-j with B5035 'Wirksworth B5035, Matlock (B5036)'

16 SA at X-road with B5023 'Crich B5035, Cromford, Matlock (B5036)' (**Or** to return to Wirksworth, turn R at X-roads 'Wirksworth, Duffield B5023', go under overbridge and descend hill to return to the start by reverse of outward route)

17 L at T-j with B5036 (NS)

18 R Derby Road 'Whatstandwell, Ambergate' at junction with A6, then L Mill Road 'Lea, Holloway, Crich', cross Cromford Bridge and bear R into Lea Road 'Crich, Holloway', then L up station drive to return to start

! Take care not to mistake the faded yellow line of the national park boundary for the solid yellow line of the route

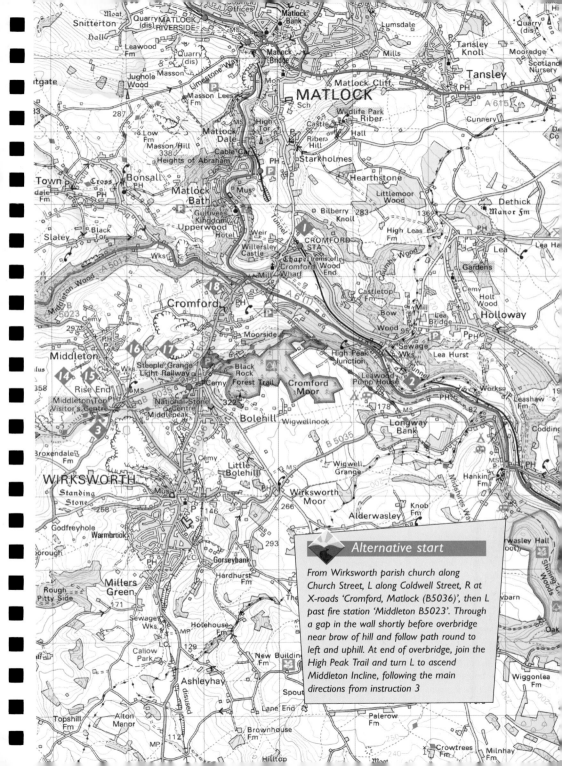

Alternative start

From Wirksworth parish church along Church Street, L along Coldwell Street, R at X-roads 'Cromford, Matlock (B5036)', then L past fire station 'Middleton B5023'. Through a gap in the wall shortly before overbridge near brow of hill and follow path round to left and uphill. At end of overbridge, join the High Peak Trail and turn L to ascend Middleton Incline, following the main directions from instruction 3

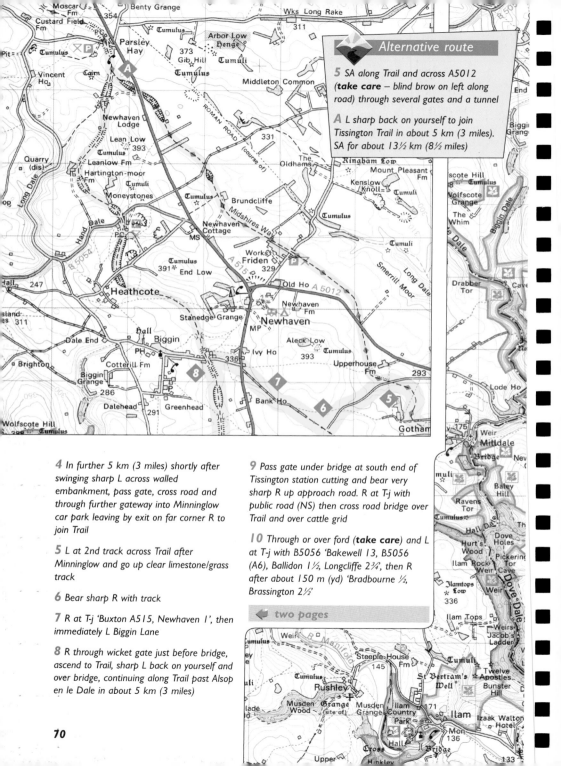

4 In further 5 km (3 miles) shortly after swinging sharp L across walled embankment, pass gate, cross road and through further gateway into Minninglow car park leaving by exit on far corner R to join Trail

5 L at 2nd track across Trail after Minninglow and go up clear limestone/grass track

6 Bear sharp R with track

7 R at T-j 'Buxton A515, Newhaven 1', then immediately L Biggin Lane

8 R through wicket gate just before bridge, ascend to Trail, sharp L back on yourself and over bridge, continuing along Trail past Alsop en le Dale in about 5 km (3 miles)

9 Pass gate under bridge at south end of Tissington station cutting and bear very sharp R up approach road. R at T-j with public road (NS) then cross road bridge over Trail and over cattle grid

10 Through or over ford (**take care**) and L at T-j with B5056 'Bakewell 13, B5056 (A6), Ballidon 1½, Longcliffe 2¾', then R after about 150 m (yd) 'Bradbourne ½, Brassington 2½'

⇐ two pages

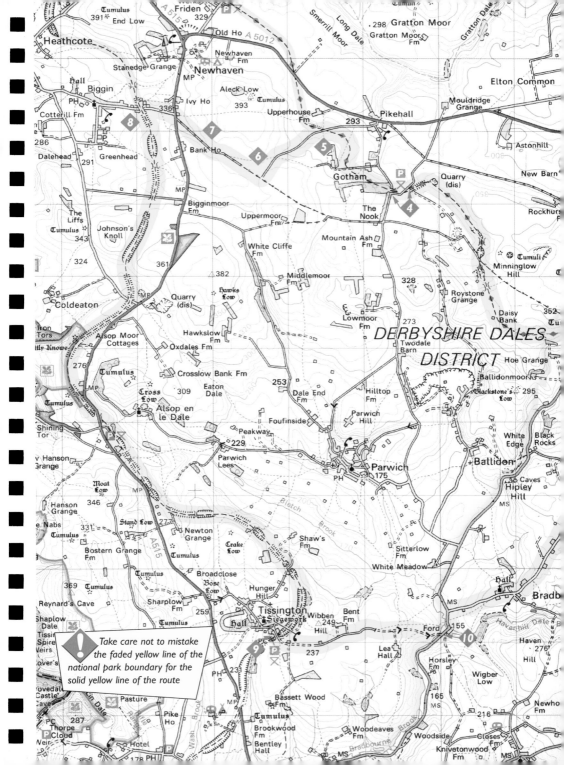

Take care not to mistake
the faded yellow line of the
national park boundary for the
solid yellow line of the route

12 Ilam, Hartington and Parwich

A ride with much to offer, no single out-standing feature, but several contrasting landscapes. The route runs across the plateau between the Dove and Manifold valleys, exploring the moorland to the west, the open countryside between Longnor and Hartington, and finally going off-road, against the lie of the land, to Kniveton and returning to Ashbourne.

76   77

74   Ashbourne   75

Start

Tourist Information Centre, Market Square, Ashbourne

P Extensive long-term parking in Ashbourne and the cycle hire centre there

Distance and grade

54 km (34 miles)
Moderate

Terrain

This is a ride that is rarely level, but does not require anything like as much effort as might be imagined. Climbs from Ilam and out of the Manifold Valley are quite steep – there is a lengthy rise from Elkstone and a short off-road rise after Tissington

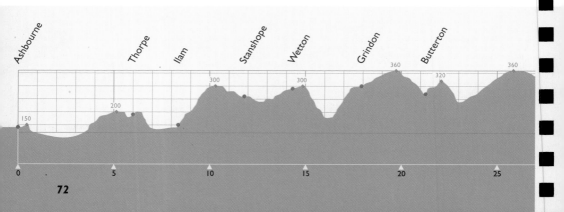

Ashbourne   Thorpe   Ilam   Stanshope   Wetton   Grindon   Butterton

150   200   300   300   360   320   360

0   5   10   15   20   25

Nearest railway

Uttoxeter, 19 km
(12 miles) from start
Derby, 22 km
(14 miles) from start
Buxton, 14 km
(9 miles) from
instruction 21

Places of interest

Hartington 27
A Cavendish manor that is now a favourite
place for day visitors. The 13th-century St
Giles' church has similarities to Wirksworth's.
The market was chartered in 1203 and the
large Market Place retains the village mere.
There is a rustic classical market hall of 1811,
and the youth hostel (up the road towards
Biggin) is an attractive, early Jacobean stone
building. The village is now one of the places
where Stilton cheese is made

Refreshments

Plenty of choice in **Ashbourne**
Tea room at **Ilam Hall**
Watts-Russell Arms, **Hopedale**
PH, cafe at craft centre in **Wetton**
Cavalier PH, **Grindon**
Shop and PH in **Butterton**
Old Butchers Arms, **Reaps Moor**
Plenty of choice in **Hartington**
Shop and PH in **Parwich**

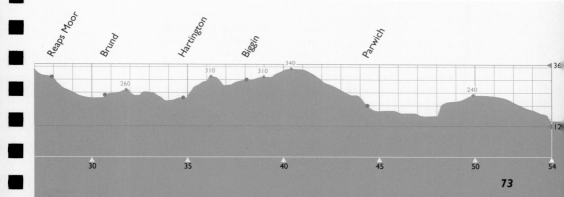

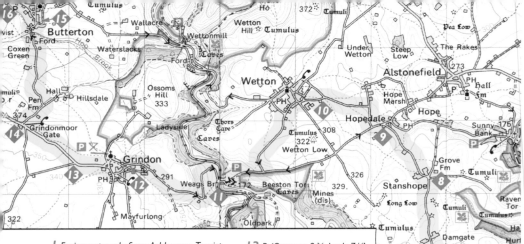

1 Facing outwards from Ashbourne Tourist Information Centre, R across Market Place towards Buxton Road where L and immediately L again into Union Street. R into Dove House Green

2 2nd L (in effect SA) Mappleton Lane

3 SA in Mappleton 'Thorpe 2¼, Dovedale'

4 L at T-j (NS)

5 Easy to miss 1st L into narrow lane between stone gateposts

6 L at T-j and immediately bear R 'Dovedale, Ilam 1½ **NB** cattle grid without warning sign on steep descent

7 R at T-j in Ilam village 'Alstonefield 3½, Wetton 4'

8 Bear L at Stanshope

9 L at T-j 'Wetton 1, Manifold Valley 1½', then immediately bear sharp R, then L to enter Wetton

10 R 'Wetton Mill 1¼, Manifold Valley, Butterton 2½' then L 'Grindon 2½, Manifold Valley' and bear L 'Single Track Road with Passing Places' in Wetton. R at T-j (**Take care** – very steep descent)

11 SA across bridge and X-roads with Manifold Track at Weags Bridge, then climb out of valley (**Take care** at junction)

12 Bear L at entry to Grindon, R at Cavalier PH, then L at triangular junction

13 R 'Onecote 2¾, Leek 7½'

14 R at T-j (in effect SA) 'Onecote 2¼, Warslow 3¾, Leek 7', then shortly R 'Butterton 1'

15 Go through ford on entering Butterton (**take care**) keep bearing L as you rise, then L at T-j 'Onecote 2¼, Warslow 2½'

➡ *three pages*

33 Enter Parwich and bear R down from Parwich Hall, then L with village shop facing you, pass village green and church on your left and SA 'Ballidon 1¾, Ashbourne 6¾'

34 Bear R on leaving Parwich

35 R at T-j 'Ballidon 1, Ashbourne 6'

36 R at T-j 'Ashbourne 5½ B5056 (A515); Fenny Bentley 3¼'

37 After 1 km (¾ mile), almost opposite turning to right 'Ford', L through gate and climb up track. Through further gate into open field at top of hill and bear R through gate near farm buildings (**not** gate SA). Through several more gates to T-j with road in Knivetonwood where R

38 R at T-j 'Ashbourne B5035'

39 After 2 km (1¼ miles) fork R

40 L at X-roads at end of Mill Road and descend Buxton Road to Market Place (2nd R) to return to start

Take care not to mistake the faded yellow line of the national park boundary for the solid yellow line of the route

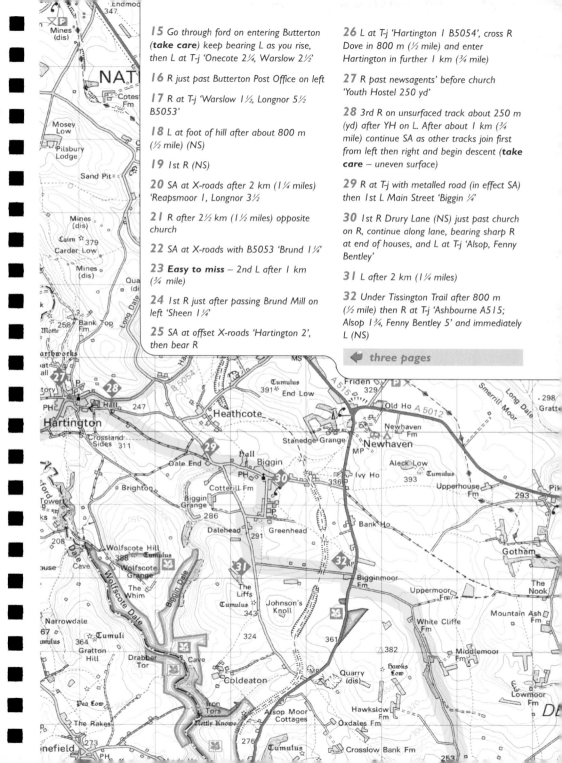

15 Go through ford on entering Butterton (**take care**) keep bearing L as you rise, then L at T-j 'Onecote 2¼, Warslow 2½'

16 R just past Butterton Post Office on left

17 R at T-j 'Warslow 1½, Longnor 5½ B5053'

18 L at foot of hill after about 800 m (½ mile) (NS)

19 1st R (NS)

20 SA at X-roads after 2 km (1¼ miles) 'Reapsmoor 1, Longnor 3½

21 R after 2½ km (1½ miles) opposite church

22 SA at X-roads with B5053 'Brund 1¼'

23 **Easy to miss** – 2nd L after 1 km (¾ mile)

24 1st R just after passing Brund Mill on left 'Sheen 1¼'

25 SA at offset X-roads 'Hartington 2', then bear R

26 L at T-j 'Hartington 1 B5054', cross R Dove in 800 m (½ mile) and enter Hartington in further 1 km (¾ mile)

27 R past newsagents' before church 'Youth Hostel 250 yd'

28 3rd R on unsurfaced track about 250 m (yd) after YH on L. After about 1 km (¾ mile) continue SA as other tracks join first from left then right and begin descent (**take care** – uneven surface)

29 R at T-j with metalled road (in effect SA) then 1st L Main Street 'Biggin ¼'

30 1st R Drury Lane (NS) just past church on R, continue along lane, bearing sharp R at end of houses, and L at T-j 'Alsop, Fenny Bentley'

31 L after 2 km (1¼ miles)

32 Under Tissington Trail after 800 m (½ mile) then R at T-j 'Ashbourne A515; Alsop 1¾, Fenny Bentley 5' and immediately L (NS)

three pages

The Dove and the Manifold valleys

This ride goes south along the Dove Valley, then heads for Waterhouses and the Manifold Track. It then crosses the plateau to Alstonefield and down to Milldale before joining the Tissington Trail to return to Ashbourne. The going on the old railway lines is easy. There are good views west from the Clifton to Snelston Road across the Dove Valley and on the road from Hulme End to Alstonefield. Be wary of quarry traffic between Ellastone and Waterhouses.

Start

Tourist Information Centre, Market Square, Ashbourne

P Extensive long-term parking in Ashbourne and the cycle hire centre there

Distance and grade

56 km (35 miles)

Easy/moderate

▼ Dovedale

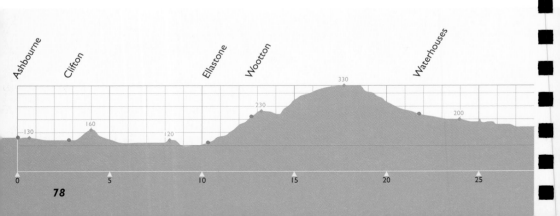

Ashbourne

Clifton

Ellastone

Wootton

Waterhouses

330

230

160

200

130

120

0   5   10   15   20   25

Terrain

The climb from Ellastone to Cauldon Lowe and an easier one from Hulme End to Alstonefield are followed by enjoyable descents. From Milldale up to the Tissington Trail is steep but short

Nearest railway

Uttoxeter, 19 km (12 miles) from start Derby 22 km (14 miles) from start

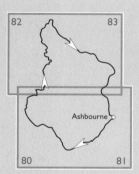

82   83

Ashbourne

80   81

Places of interest

Dovedale and the River Dove *19*
Dovedale is one of the great 'draws' of the Peak. The river rises on Axe Edge and flows east of Longnor down to Hartington through an attractive farming valley. The gorge, running south of Hartington as far as Ilam, has famous features that are mostly accessible only on foot – neither road nor bridleway runs down the bottom of the valley. The only section of the Dove Gorge that can be cycled lies between Milldale and Shining Tor

Cauldon *12/13*
The quarries on the right along the descent to Waterhouses were formerly operated by the local railway and the intended foundation stone for the new Euston station was quarried here by way of a remotely controlled explosion set off in London in 1938

Refreshments

Plenty of choice in **Ashbourne**
Duncombe Arms, **Ellastone**
Yew Tree Inn, **Cauldon**
Shop, pubs and cycle hire centre at **Waterhouses**
Teas at Lea House Farm and Wettonmill along **Manifold Track**
Manifold Valley Hotel, **Hulme End**
George and Dragon PH, **Alstonefield**
Shop in **Milldale**
Tea room in **Tissington**
Cycle hire centre, at end of **Tissington Trail**

Hulme End   Alestonefield   Tissington

300   270   240   33

200   150

10

30   35   40   45   50   55 56

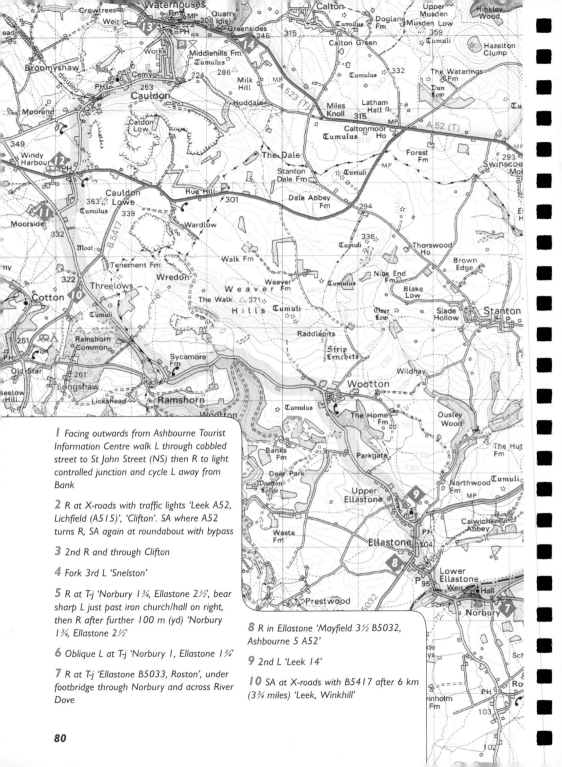

1 Facing outwards from Ashbourne Tourist Information Centre walk L through cobbled street to St John Street (NS) then R to light controlled junction and cycle L away from Bank

2 R at X-roads with traffic lights 'Leek A52, Lichfield (A515)', 'Clifton'. SA where A52 turns R, SA again at roundabout with bypass

3 2nd R and through Clifton

4 Fork 3rd L 'Snelston'

5 R at T-j 'Norbury 1¾, Ellastone 2½, bear sharp L just past iron church/hall on right, then R after further 100 m (yd) 'Norbury 1¾, Ellastone 2½'

6 Oblique L at T-j 'Norbury 1, Ellastone 1¾'

7 R at T-j 'Ellastone B5033, Roston', under footbridge through Norbury and across River Dove

8 R in Ellastone 'Mayfield 3½ B5032, Ashbourne 5 A52'

9 2nd L 'Leek 14'

10 SA at X-roads with B5417 after 6 km (3¾ miles) 'Leek, Winkhill'

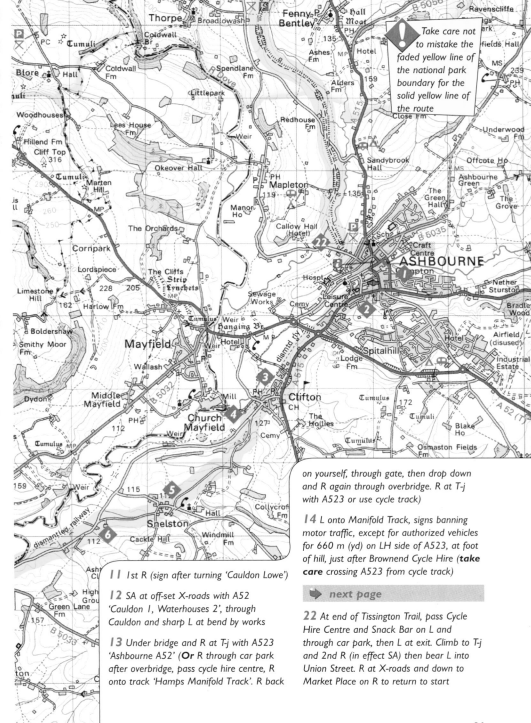

Take care not to mistake the faded yellow line of the national park boundary for the solid yellow line of the route

11 1st R (sign after turning 'Cauldon Lowe')

12 SA at off-set X-roads with A52 'Cauldon 1, Waterhouses 2', through Cauldon and sharp L at bend by works

13 Under bridge and R at T-j with A523 'Ashbourne A52' (**Or** R through car park after overbridge, pass cycle hire centre, R onto track 'Hamps Manifold Track'. R back

on yourself, through gate, then drop down and R again through overbridge. R at T-j with A523 or use cycle track)

14 L onto Manifold Track, signs banning motor traffic, except for authorized vehicles for 660 m (yd) on LH side of A523, at foot of hill, just after Brownend Cycle Hire (**take care** crossing A523 from cycle track)

➡ next page

22 At end of Tissington Trail, pass Cycle Hire Centre and Snack Bar on L and through car park, then L at exit. Climb to T-j and 2nd R (in effect SA) then bear L into Union Street. R at X-roads and down to Market Place on R to return to start

13 Under bridge and R at T-j with A523 'Ashbourne A52' (**Or** R through car park after overbridge, pass cycle hire centre, R onto track 'Hamps Manifold Track'. R back on yourself, through gate, then drop down and R again through overbridge. R at T-j with A523 or use cycle track)

14 L onto Manifold Track, signs banning motor traffic, except for authorized vehicles for 660 m (yd) on LH side of A523, at foot of hill, just after Brownend Cycle Hire (**take care** crossing A523 from cycle track)

15 SA at X-roads after 5 km (3 miles) by Weag's Bridge. **Take care** – no 'Give Way' signs

16 After 3 km (1¾ miles) SA at X-roads at Wettonmill 'Hulme End 2¾'. Manifold Track is open to motor vehicles for next 2 km (1¼ miles). SA past 'No motor vehicles' sign beside gate after Swainsley tunnel. SA across road after 2 km (1¼ miles) at Ecton

! Take care not to mistake the faded yellow line of the national park boundary for the solid yellow line of the route

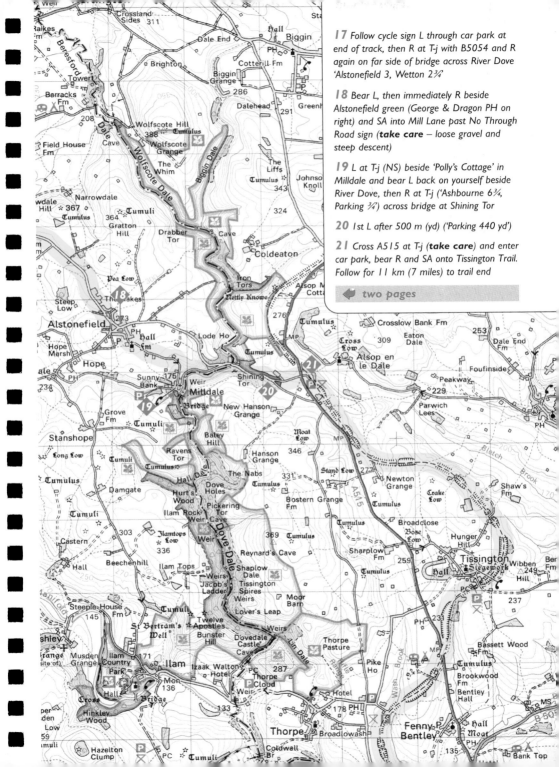

17 Follow cycle sign L through car park at end of track, then R at T-j with B5054 and R again on far side of bridge across River Dove 'Alstonefield 3, Wetton 2¾'

18 Bear L, then immediately R beside Alstonefield green (George & Dragon PH on right) and SA into Mill Lane past No Through Road sign (**take care** – loose gravel and steep descent)

19 L at T-j (NS) beside 'Polly's Cottage' in Milldale and bear L back on yourself beside River Dove, then R at T-j ('Ashbourne 6¾, Parking ¾') across bridge at Shining Tor

20 1st L after 500 m (yd) ('Parking 440 yd')

21 Cross A515 at T-j (**take care**) and enter car park, bear R and SA onto Tissington Trail. Follow for 11 km (7 miles) to trail end

◀ two pages

14 *Old Roads around Buxton*

This route explores the White Peak around Buxton. It follows the line of several old packhorse routes and turnpikes and offers excellent views on fine days. Conspicuous hills on either side of Dowel Dale – on the left bank of Upper Dovedale – are classically hill-shaped (almost unique in the Peak District). This is because they are formed from reef limestone, which is harder than the carboniferous kind, which underlies most of the White Peak and resisted the effects of glaciation.

Refreshments

Plenty of choice in Buxton
Plenty of choice in Longnor
Waterloo PH at crossing of A6 west of Taddington
Angler's Rest PH, Miller's Dale
Plenty of choice in Tideswell
PH in Smalldale
Midland Hotel, Peak Dale

Start

Buxton Tourist Information Centre, The Crescent

P Various public car parks in Buxton

Distance and grade

42 km (26 miles)

 Moderate/strenuous

Terrain

Unsealed former turnpike roads, grass bridleways and farm tracks. Long off-road climb out of Buxton, and shorter on-road climbs out of Dovedale, from Miller's Dale and up to Wheston. Some stretches of bridleway are deeply rutted

Nearest railway

Buxton

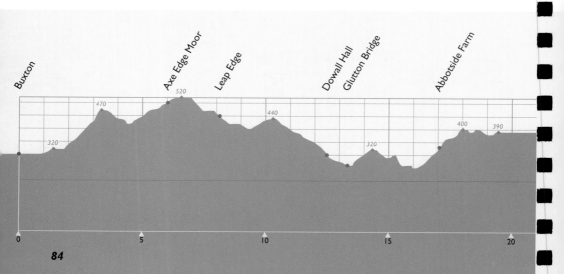

Buxton /

One of the centres of the Peak. It began as a spa on the boundary between the limestone and the millstone grit, where water emerged from the ground at 28° C (82° F). The Romans had a bathing station (Aquae Arnemetiae) and many routes converged on it. Mary Queen of Scots sought here the cure for her rheumatism. The town was originally around the Market Place but expanded downhill in the 18th-century when the 5th Duke of Devonshire resolved to create a northern rival to Bath. The Crescent was built in the 1780s, followed by stables that were converted into the Devonshire Royal Hospital in 1859. The Pump Room opposite is now a Micrarium where you may see the universe at microscopic level, St Ann's Cliff and gardens behind and above it. The Museum in Terrace Road contains much material found in the High Peak

▶ The River Wye

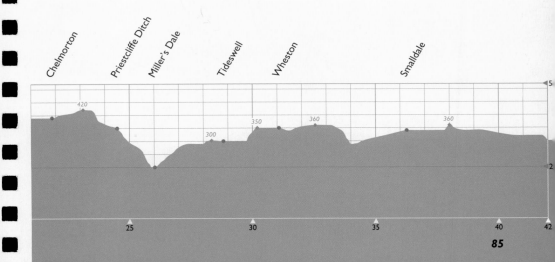

as you look out from Buxton Tourist mation Centre along Hartington Road

at T-j Bath Road, then R again at further T-j Macclesfield Road (NS)

3 SA at traffic lights into Macclesfield Old Road (**take care**). Continue along road as it climbs (becomes a stony track). Pass through several gates

➡ **two pages**

20 SA at X-roads with A6

21 L at further X-roads 'Priestcliffe Ditch, Blackwell, Miller's Dale' and R along track after further 200 m (yd) (in effect SA) 'Limestone Way'

22 R at T-j onto B6049 (**take care**)

23 L after church 'Unsuitable for Motor Vehicles'

24 In Tideswell R beside United Reform Church, then L at T-j and bear L into High Street

25 L up Wheston Bank

26 R in Wheston, then bear L

27 L in 2 km (1¼ mile) down track 'Limestone Way' bearing L down into Dam Dale, then sharp R with track

28 SA at X-roads 'Smalldale 1¼'

29 L in Smalldale 'Peak Dale ½, Batham Gate 1'

30 L at far end of Batham Gate, just before A6, 'Water Swallows ½'

31 R 'Dove Holes 2½, Buxton 2½'

⚠️ Take care not to mistake the faded yellow line of the national park boundary for the solid yellow line of the route

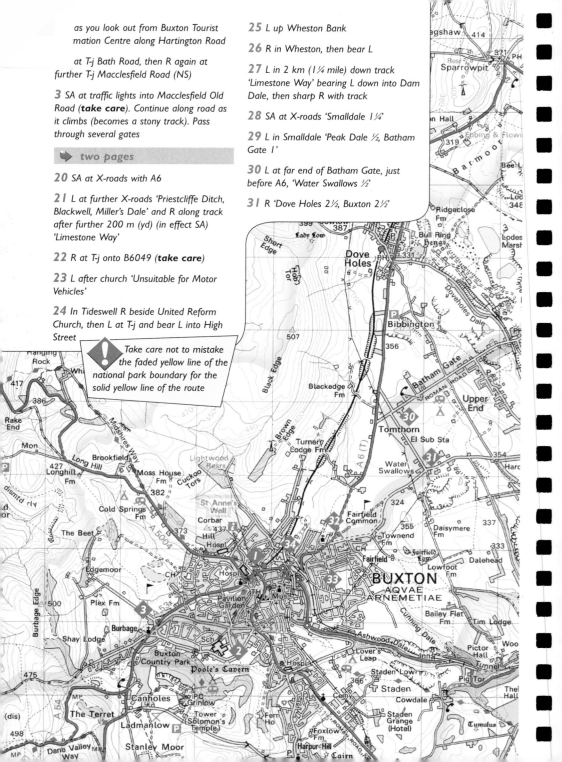

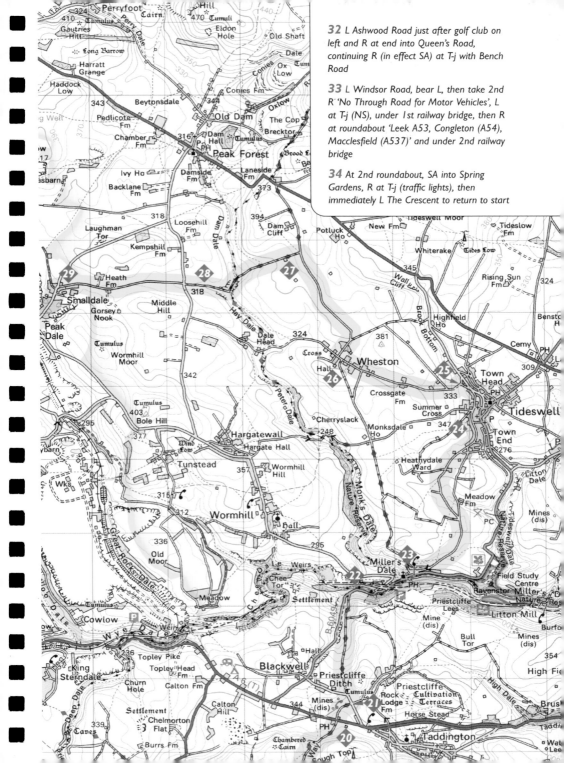

32 L Ashwood Road just after golf club on left and R at end into Queen's Road, continuing R (in effect SA) at T-j with Bench Road

33 L Windsor Road, bear L, then take 2nd R 'No Through Road for Motor Vehicles', L at T-j (NS), under 1st railway bridge, then R at roundabout 'Leek A53, Congleton (A54), Macclesfield (A537)' and under 2nd railway bridge

34 At 2nd roundabout, SA into Spring Gardens, R at T-j (traffic lights), then immediately L The Crescent to return to start

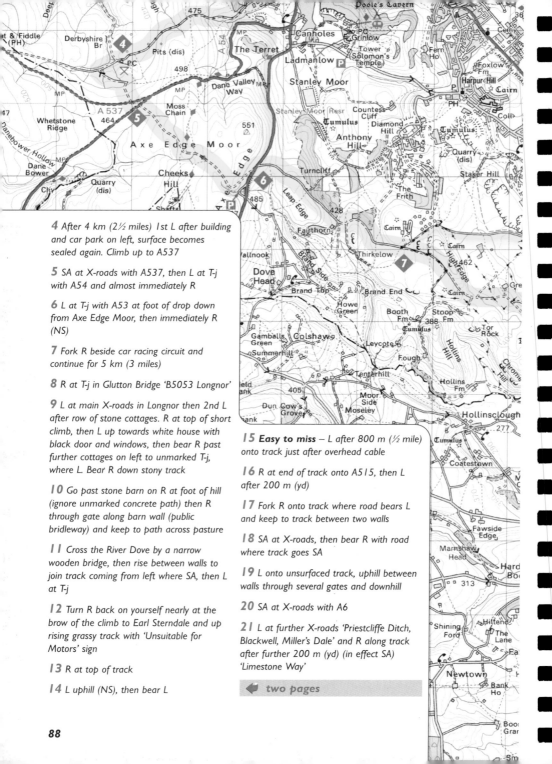

4 After 4 km (2½ miles) 1st L after building and car park on left, surface becomes sealed again. Climb up to A537

5 SA at X-roads with A537, then L at T-j with A54 and almost immediately R

6 L at T-j with A53 at foot of drop down from Axe Edge Moor, then immediately R (NS)

7 Fork R beside car racing circuit and continue for 5 km (3 miles)

8 R at T-j in Glutton Bridge 'B5053 Longnor'

9 L at main X-roads in Longnor then 2nd L after row of stone cottages. R at top of short climb, then L up towards white house with black door and windows, then bear R past further cottages on left to unmarked T-j, where L. Bear R down stony track

10 Go past stone barn on R at foot of hill (ignore unmarked concrete path) then R through gate along barn wall (public bridleway) and keep to path across pasture

11 Cross the River Dove by a narrow wooden bridge, then rise between walls to join track coming from left where SA, then L at T-j

12 Turn R back on yourself nearly at the brow of the climb to Earl Sterndale and up rising grassy track with 'Unsuitable for Motors' sign

13 R at top of track

14 L uphill (NS), then bear L

15 **Easy to miss** – L after 800 m (½ mile) onto track just after overhead cable

16 R at end of track onto A515, then L after 200 m (yd)

17 Fork R onto track where road bears L and keep to track between two walls

18 SA at X-roads, then bear R with road where track goes SA

19 L onto unsurfaced track, uphill between walls through several gates and downhill

20 SA at X-roads with A6

21 L at further X-roads 'Priestcliffe Ditch, Blackwell, Miller's Dale' and R along track after further 200 m (yd) (in effect SA) 'Limestone Way'

◀ two pages

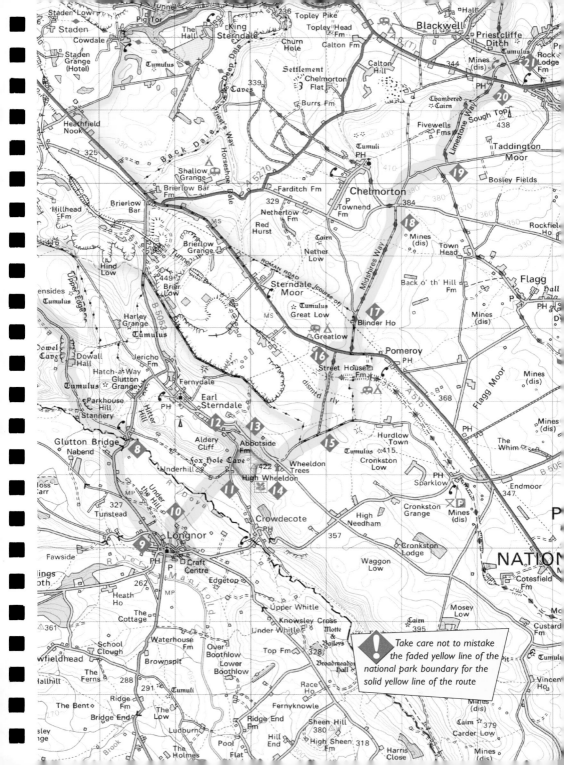

Take care not to mistake the faded yellow line of the national park boundary for the solid yellow line of the route

Around the Derwent Reservoirs

15

These are mainly off-road routes that join each other to offer alternative rides from Fairholmes (between the Derwent and Ladybower reservoirs). The Upper Derwent Valley has been dammed in the course of the last hundred years and three reservoirs now fill it and the Woodlands Valley to the west. It is a popular area but the National Park has imposed traffic restrictions at the busiest times and there are many opportunities for off-road and virtually traffic-free cycling.

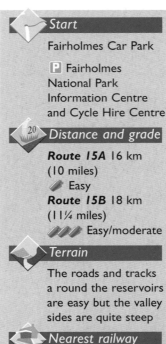

Start

Fairholmes Car Park

P Fairholmes National Park Information Centre and Cycle Hire Centre

Distance and grade

Route 15A 16 km (10 miles)
🛡 Easy
Route 15B 18 km (11¼ miles)
🛡🛡🛡 Easy/moderate

Terrain

The roads and tracks around the reservoirs are easy but the valley sides are quite steep

Nearest railway

Hope and Bamford

Refreshments

Drinks and snacks are available at Fairholmes Visitor Centre, and sometimes near the phone box below the Derwent Dam on the east side of **Ladybower Reservoir**
Ladybower Inn (on A57 east of instruction 4 on Route 15B)
The Yorkshire Bridge PH

Route 15A

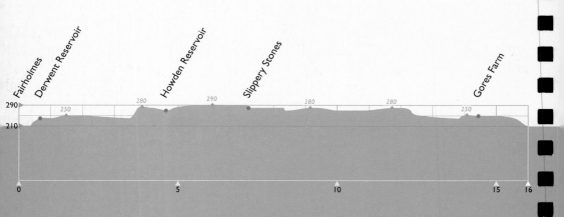

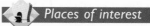
Places of interest

The Derwent Valley

The upper Derwent Valley was remote and sparsely populated when the growing demand for water in the industrial cities of the East Midlands brought about the construction of the great stone dams, to hold back the Howden and Derwent Reservoirs, in the years before the Great War. Increased need for water brought about a third, earth dam at Yorkshire Bridge, retaining Ladybower Reservoir and inaugurated by King George VI in 1945. This time, the villages of Ashop and Derwent were submerged. The two stone dams were among those used for practice flying by the RAF in preparation for the dambuster raids in the Ruhr valleys, where the dams were similar in design

◀ Derwent Dam

Route 15B

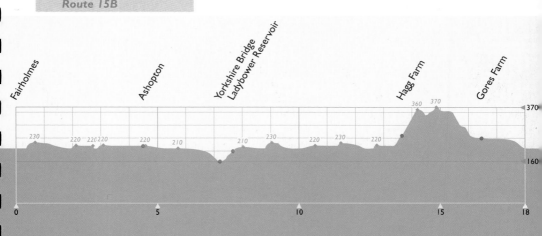

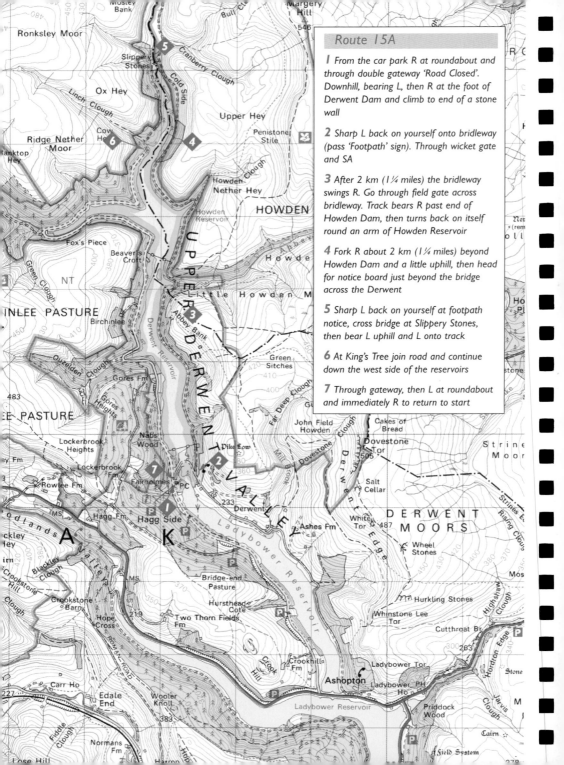

Route 15A

1 From the car park R at roundabout and through double gateway 'Road Closed'. Downhill, bearing L, then R at the foot of Derwent Dam and climb to end of a stone wall

2 Sharp L back on yourself onto bridleway (pass 'Footpath' sign). Through wicket gate and SA

3 After 2 km (1¼ miles) the bridleway swings R. Go through field gate across bridleway. Track bears R past end of Howden Dam, then turns back on itself round an arm of Howden Reservoir

4 Fork R about 2 km (1¼ miles) beyond Howden Dam and a little uphill, then head for notice board just beyond the bridge across the Derwent

5 Sharp L back on yourself at footpath notice, cross bridge at Slippery Stones, then bear L uphill and L onto track

6 At King's Tree join road and continue down the west side of the reservoirs

7 Through gateway, then L at roundabout and immediately R to return to start

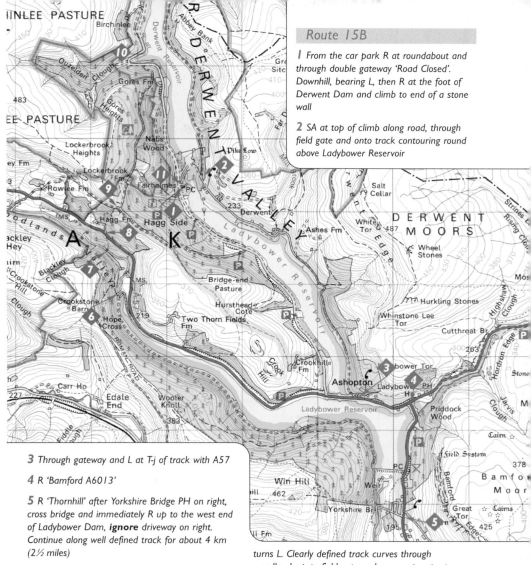

Route 15B

1 From the car park R at roundabout and through double gateway 'Road Closed'. Downhill, bearing L, then R at the foot of Derwent Dam and climb to end of a stone wall

2 SA at top of climb along road, through field gate and onto track contouring round above Ladybower Reservoir

3 Through gateway and L at T-j of track with A57

4 R 'Bamford A6013'

5 R 'Thornhill' after Yorkshire Bridge PH on right, cross bridge and immediately R up to the west end of Ladybower Dam, **ignore** driveway on right. Continue along well defined track for about 4 km (2½ miles)

6 Fork obliquely L (**not** sharp L) by metal bridge. **Walk** up to field gate with stile across path (this is a footpath, the gate is locked and your bike will have to be lifted over it)

7 Obliquely R immediately after passing over gate, down bridleway bearing L, then sharp R across stream and uphill again between walls

8 Through gate, across A57 up drive to Hagg Farm 'Derwent Dale 1½', then SA up track where drive

turns L. Clearly defined track curves through woodland, up to field gate and across open pasture

9 SA at crossing of bridleways 'Lockerbrook, Derwent Reservoir', then along track and through several gates and into woods where track bears sharp L downhill, then R back on itself (you can see the road not far away below)

10 R at T-j with tarmacked road (NS)

11 Through gateway, then L at roundabout and immediately R to return to the start

93

Houndkirk, Stanedge Pole and Abney

16

Mixes of quiet roads, unmaintained county roads and bridleways across moorland and rivers. On the road from Fox House towards Hathersage is Surprise View from which the valley of the Derwent and Noe rivers beyond are a magnificent sight. To the north of the road is Carl Wark, a great hill fort – it may be Iron Age, post-Roman or a mixture of both. Stanage Edge is a popular area for walkers and climbers and the track crossing it was once a packhorse way.

Start

Hathersage Station
P Off Oddfellows Road, Hathersage

Distance and grade

35 km (22 miles)
(22 km (14 miles) if returning direct to Hathersage from instruction 11)
Moderate

Terrain

The sections from Grindleford to Fox House, off-road from Redmires up to Stanedge Pole and again from Brough to Abney need some effort and the descent of Stanage Edge needs care – none are too difficult

Nearest railway

Edale, Grindleford, Hathersage and Hope

Refreshments

The Yorkshire Bridge PH
Plenty of choice in **Hathersage**
Station cafe, **Grindleford**
Fox House Inn
Norfolk Arms, **Ringinglow**
Several pubs and shop in **Bamford**
Traveller PH, **Brough**
Greyhound PH, **Leadmill**

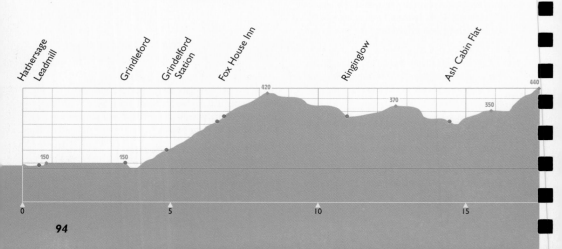

Longshaw 2/3
The Longshaw Estate, once a shooting ground of the Manners family, is now in the hands of the National Trust. There are over 600 ha (1,500 acres) of woodland and open moor with extensive footpaths, well worth exploring

Fox House and Houndkirk 3
Houndkirk Road, rising to almost 430 m (1400 ft), used to be the turnpike route linking Grindleford and Hathersage with Sheffield and may have Roman or earlier origins. It was replaced in 1812 by the Duke of Devonshire. Fox House was constructed by a Mr Fox (a local landowner) as the destination for his constitutionals and subsequently became a staging point for coaches. Charlotte Brontë is claimed to have had Fox House in mind as the alighting point for Jane Eyre on her flight to Morton/Hathersage

▼ *Bole Hill, Eyam Moor*

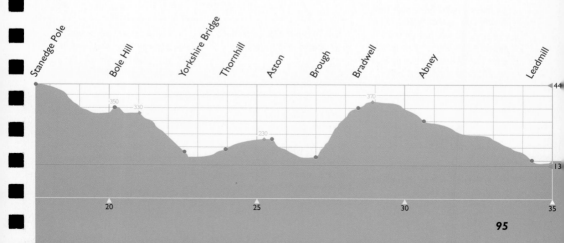

1 L from Hathersage Station road exit onto B6001, passing under the railway bridge and SA to Grindleford

2 L at T-j onto B6521 'Sheffield 9½ (A625)'

3 R at T-j and bear L round Fox House Inn, both 'Sheffield 8 A625'

4 L onto track (where A625 bears R) 'Public Byway'. SA (ignore Field Centre access track after 1 km (¾ mile) on left) and pass through wicket gate by locked field gate. Bear slightly R and ignore footpath on left. Cross a bridleway and uphill short distance. Cross stream (parapet on the R only) and head for another wicket gate by field gate. Continue SA and downhill

5 L onto road

6 L at T-j opposite Norfolk Arms PH in Ringinglow, then immediately R into Fulwood Lane

7 L at T-j Brown Hills Lane and sharp R after 400 m (yd)

8 L at further T-j and rise past the Redmires Reservoirs

9 At end of tarmac, R uphill beside wall along track 'Public Byway', to Stanedge Pole

10 Bear R after pole along well-defined track beside fence R (surface deteriorates). At fork bear L, descending along track

11 SA where track meets road below Stanage Edge, then R after 200 m (yd) 'Ladybower' (**Or** for short cut back to Hathersage SA. Outside Hathersage L into Jagger's Lane, then L at T-j and R onto B6001 'Grindleford 3, Baslow 5' to return to station)

12 L at T-j with A6013, then immediately R 'Thornhill' to cross River Derwent

13 Bear L immediately after bridge

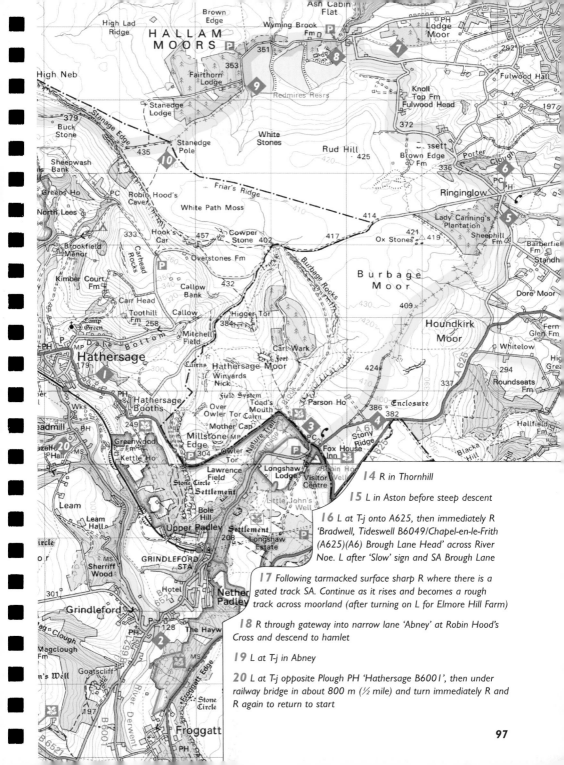

14 R in Thornhill

15 L in Aston before steep descent

16 L at T-j onto A625, then immediately R 'Bradwell, Tideswell B6049/Chapel-en-le-Frith (A625)(A6) Brough Lane Head' across River Noe. L after 'Slow' sign and SA Brough Lane

17 Following tarmacked surface sharp R where there is a gated track SA. Continue as it rises and becomes a rough track across moorland (after turning on L for Elmore Hill Farm)

18 R through gateway into narrow lane 'Abney' at Robin Hood's Cross and descend to hamlet

19 L at T-j in Abney

20 L at T-j opposite Plough PH 'Hathersage B6001', then under railway bridge in about 800 m (½ mile) and turn immediately R and R again to return to start

17 From Castleton to Great Hucklow, returning by the River Noe

A short route passing Mam Tor, the shivering mountain, that is made up of alternating layers of shale and firmer rock. Mam Tor has had repeated landslips and the old turnpike road closed to motor traffic twenty years ago following major subsidence. The ride continues over Old Moor to the Hucklows and Offerton – a small hamlet with some fascinating stone houses dating from the 16th and 17th-centuries.

Refreshments

*Plenty of choice in **Castleton***
*Queen Anne PH, **Great Hucklow***
*Traveller PH, **Brough***
*Pubs, cafes and tea rooms in **Hope***

 ## Start

Tourist Information Centre, Castleton

P Pay and display car park on north side of A625 in Castleton

 ## Distance and grade

27 km (17 miles)
Moderate

Terrain

The start of the route over the old Mam Tor road is not hard but you may need to dismount to pass some of the landslides. The high level stretch from Mam Tor to Offerton is easy, though you should keep a look out for quarry traffic. The descent from Offerton, on large cobbles, requires care in wet weather

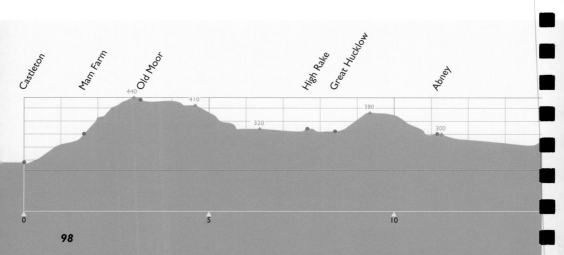

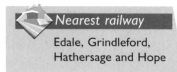

Nearest railway

Edale, Grindleford, Hathersage and Hope

Places of interest

Castleton 1

Here, the Normans created their power centre in the Peak, and the remains of Peveril Castle still dominates the village. Later, the extraction of minerals became the principal activity and several old mines now complement the natural caverns open to the public. One of the major 'honeypots' of the National Park

▼ Neae Mam Tor

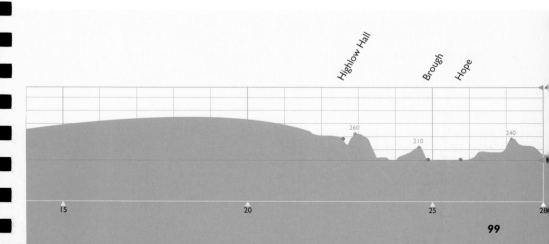

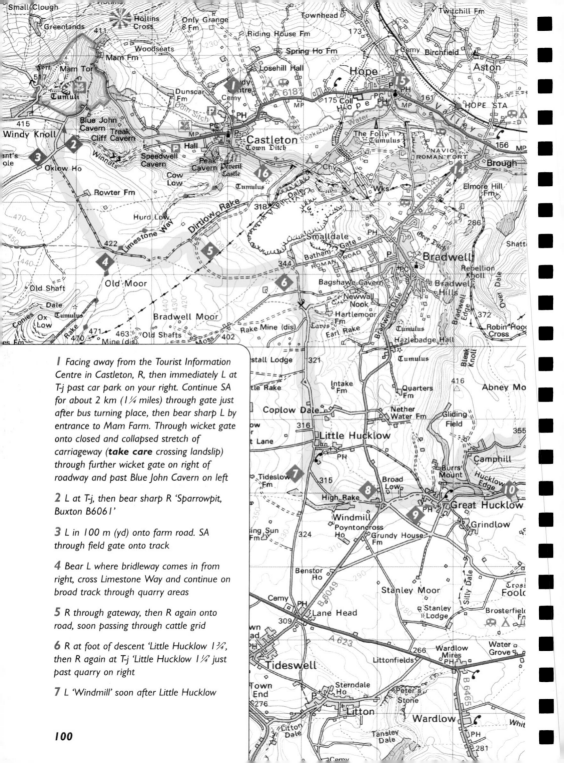

1 Facing away from the Tourist Information
Centre in Castleton, R, then immediately L at
T-j past car park on your right. Continue SA
for about 2 km (1¼ miles) through gate just
after bus turning place, then bear sharp L by
entrance to Mam Farm. Through wicket gate
onto closed and collapsed stretch of
carriageway (**take care** crossing landslip)
through further wicket gate on right of
roadway and past Blue John Cavern on left

2 L at T-j, then bear sharp R 'Sparrowpit,
Buxton B6061'

3 L in 100 m (yd) onto farm road. SA
through field gate onto track

4 Bear L where bridleway comes in from
right, cross Limestone Way and continue on
broad track through quarry areas

5 R through gateway, then R again onto
road, soon passing through cattle grid

6 R at foot of descent 'Little Hucklow 1¾',
then R again at T-j 'Little Hucklow 1¼ just
past quarry on right

7 L 'Windmill' soon after Little Hucklow

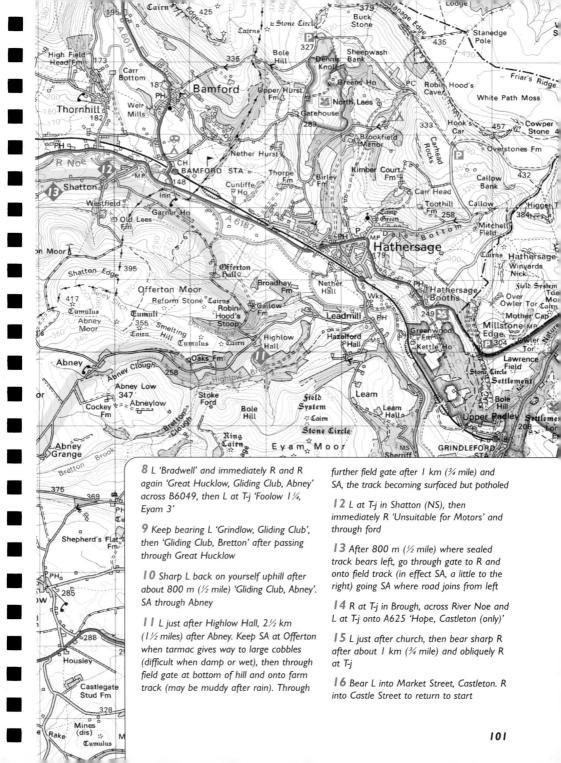

8 L 'Bradwell' and immediately R and R again 'Great Hucklow, Gliding Club, Abney' across B6049, then L at T-j 'Foolow 1¼, Eyam 3'

9 Keep bearing L 'Grindlow, Gliding Club', then 'Gliding Club, Bretton' after passing through Great Hucklow

10 Sharp L back on yourself uphill after about 800 m (½ mile) 'Gliding Club, Abney'. SA through Abney

11 L just after Highlow Hall, 2½ km (1½ miles) after Abney. Keep SA at Offerton when tarmac gives way to large cobbles (difficult when damp or wet), then through field gate at bottom of hill and onto farm track (may be muddy after rain). Through further field gate after 1 km (¾ mile) and SA, the track becoming surfaced but potholed

12 L at T-j in Shatton (NS), then immediately R 'Unsuitable for Motors' and through ford

13 After 800 m (½ mile) where sealed track bears left, go through gate to R and onto field track (in effect SA, a little to the right) going SA where road joins from left

14 R at T-j in Brough, across River Noe and L at T-j onto A625 'Hope, Castleton (only)'

15 L just after church, then bear sharp R after about 1 km (¾ mile) and obliquely R at T-j

16 Bear L into Market Street, Castleton. R into Castle Street to return to start

From Langsett to Low Bradfield

18

An exploration of the countryside north of the Loxley Valley, encompassing more deep valleys, moorland, woods and reservoirs. The chief points of interest are the views from the high moorland roads.

Start

Langsett Youth Hostel

P Adjoining A616 west of Langsett village

Distance and grade

27 km (17 miles)

🥾🥾🥾🥾 Moderate/ strenuous

Terrain

Some taxing climbs from Ewden Bridge, up to High Bradfield, and between Broomhead Reservoir and

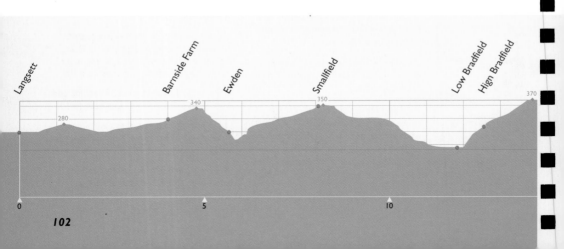

Bolsterstone, however, long sections either roughly follow contours or run downhill. The roads are fairly quiet but the steepness of the hills means that low gears and good brakes are needed

Nearest railway

Penistone 6½ km (4 miles) from Langsett, 3 km (2 miles) from Cranberry Farm

Places of interest

Broomhead Hall 4
An early 19th-century building in Tudor style, downhill to the left after Ewden Bridge

Midhopestones 19
The tiny church here, St James', is a contrast with the edifice at High Bradfield. It has relics of an earlier age in its boxed pews with parishioners' names and west gallery. A Queen Anne building, with Jacobean pulpit. Nearby is an oddly curious house, described as both homely and Palladian at the same time. Built with a three bay, three storey, pedimented central section and lower, half-pedimented wings

Refreshments

Waggon and Horses PH, cafe and shop, **Langsett**
Old Horns PH, **High Bradfield**
Castle Inn and shop, **Bolsterstone**
Midhopestones Arms, **Midhopestones**

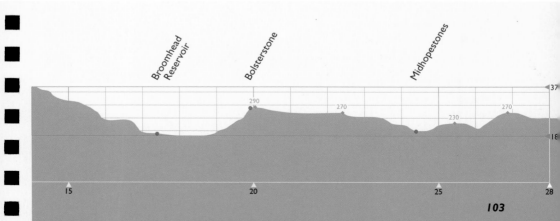

1 From Langsett Youth Hostel L at A616 (**take care**) then R at Waggon and Horses PH 'Strines, Derwentwater' and cross top of dam

2 Sharp bend R 'Strines, Derwentwater' and continue to bear L along road

3 R at T-j 'Strines, Derwentwater' shortly after forest ends on left. Take road to right, uphill over ridge, then descend to Ewden Bridge and climb (steeply at first)

4 **Ignore** turning L for Wigtwizzle, continue SA

5 Bear R diagonally uphill along unfenced road

6 L 'Bradfield, Dungworth' as road crosses ridge and contour L along mostly unfenced road

7 R at T-j downhill along ridge road to Low Bradfield and Agden Reservoir

8 L at T-j above Low Bradfield and immediately up steep hill

9 L at T-j in High Bradfield, Brown House Lane 'Bolsterstone 4¾, Midhopestones 5¾'

10 Fork R 'Midhopestones 5¼'

11 L at T-j with milestone (**take care** – sharp bends on steep hill)

12 SA at X-roads and descend towards reservoir

13 Keep SA to head of reservoir

14 Bear R round head of reservoir and R at T-j 'Bolsterstone 2, Stocksbridge 4', then bear L uphill, away from reservoir

15 L in Bolsterstone by Castle Inn 'Stocksbridge 1½, Midhopestones 2½'

16 L, then fork R in about 400 m (¼ mile)

17 Fork L at grass triangle (NS)

18 Obliquely R 'Penistone 3, Midhopestones ½'

19 L by Midhopestones Arms 'Upper Midhope 1½, then R at T-j at Upper Midhope 'Langsett ½' to return across dam to the start

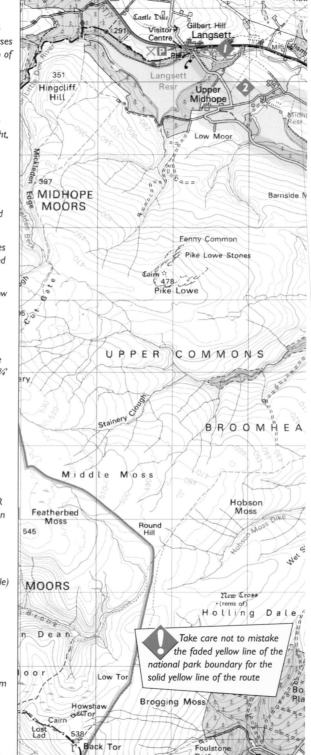

Take care not to mistake the faded yellow line of the national park boundary for the solid yellow line of the route

19 *The White Peak*

*T*hrough old mining villages in the White Peak, between the Derwent and Dove rivers, southwest of Bakewell. Quarrying is still important around Brassington and Parwich. There is little surface water in the area but the River Lathkill, below Over Haddon, and the River Bradford at Alport offer delightful riverside walks and views.

 Start

Tourist Information Centre, Bakewell Market Place

P Extensive (but busy) pay car parking in Bakewell. Car parks also at Over Haddon and along the Tissington Trail

 Distance and grade

51 km (32 miles)
Easy/moderate

 Terrain

Several sections on undulating tableland and a comfortable ascent from Parwich up to Biggin. Climbs out of the valleys of the River Wye (from Bakewell) and the River Bradford (from Alport) have sharp pitches

◀ *Lathkill Dale*

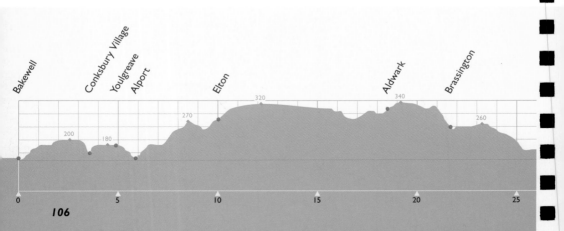

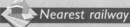
Buxton, 14 km (9 miles)
from Parsley Hay
Matlock, 10 km
(6 miles) from Elton

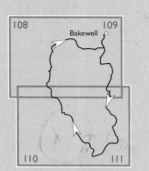

108 109
Bakewell

110 111

Refreshments

Plenty of choice in **Bakewell**
Plenty of choice in **Youlgreave**
Cafe and PH in **Elton**
Pubs in **Brassington** and **Parwich**
Snacks at **Parsley Hay**
Old Smithy and Village Stores tea rooms and
Bull's Head PH, in **Monyash**
Yew Tree tearoom, Uncle Geoff's Diner and
Craft Centre in **Over Haddon**

Places of interest

Bakewell 1

A busy town with a market on Mondays,
Bakewell was one of the traditional
administrative centres of Derbyshire and is
now the largest town and site of the main
offices of the Peak National Park. Past
Dukes of Rutland tried, but failed, to make
it a spa town like Buxton. Bakeries vie for
the right to be the only original source of
the Bakewell Pudding – the result, it seems,
of a cook getting things wrong when
making a jam tart at the Rutland Arms

Lathkill Dale 3

One of the larger parts of the Derbyshire
Dales National Nature Reserve and the
one most accessible to the
public. There is no cycle access
within the reserve but it is well
worth exploring on foot. There
is an information centre at Over
Haddon

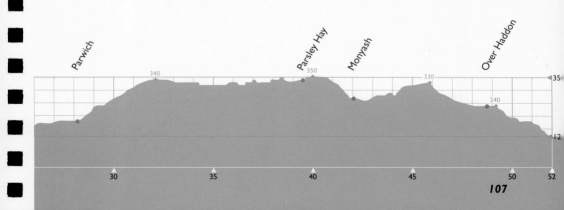

1 From Bakewell Tourist Information Centre along Bridge Street towards Rutland Arms, L at roundabout Matlock Street and immediately R King Street ('B5055 Monyash 5')

2 3rd L Yeld Road

3 L after crossing River Lathkill at Conksbury Bridge 'Youlgreave ¾'

4 L at T-j in Youlgreave (George PH on L, church SA) 'Alport ¾, Bakewell 4½'

5 R at foot of hill entering Alport, after crossing River Lathkill again. Bear L, then R at T-j (NS) and cross River Bradford

6 Sharp L at T-j 'Elton'

7 R Moor Lane in Elton

➡ **two pages**

21 After passing through cutting and joining High Peak Trail go past gate and turn back on yourself R, pass Parsley Hay Cycle Hire Centre and through car park. Turn L at exit, L again at T-j with A515, and immediately R (**take care**)

22 SA at X-roads in Monyash, then 1st R

23 R at T-j after 2½ km (1½ miles) 'Ashford 2, Bakewell 3'. **Ignore** 1st junction on left 'Ashford 1'

24 R onto stony track (clump of trees at fork)

25 SA at X-roads with B5055 'Over Haddon, Lathkilldale 1½'

26 R just after 30 mph sign on entering Over Haddon (parking sign). Bear L, L again beside Over Haddon Craft Centre, then R on leaving village 'Youlgreave 2½ (**not** SA 'Bakewell 2')

27 L at T-j 'Bakewell 1½'

28 R at T-j to return to start by reverse of outward route

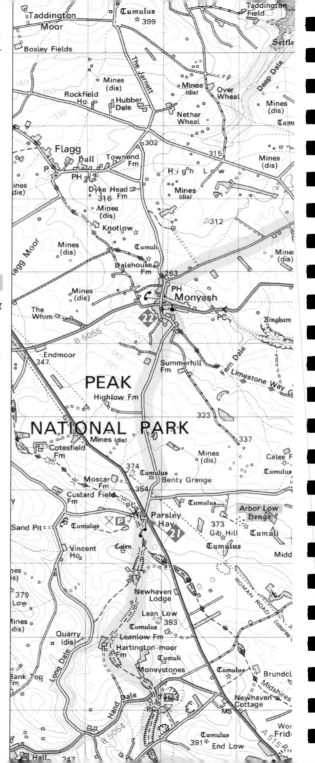

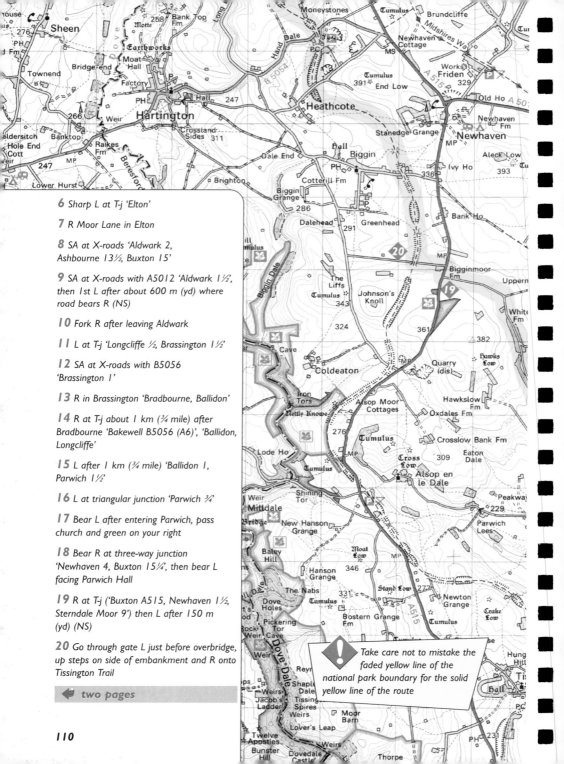

6 Sharp L at T-j 'Elton'

7 R Moor Lane in Elton

8 SA at X-roads 'Aldwark 2, Ashbourne 13½, Buxton 15'

9 SA at X-roads with A5012 'Aldwark 1½', then 1st L after about 600 m (yd) where road bears R (NS)

10 Fork R after leaving Aldwark

11 L at T-j 'Longcliffe ½, Brassington 1½'

12 SA at X-roads with B5056 'Brassington 1'

13 R in Brassington 'Bradbourne, Ballidon'

14 R at T-j about 1 km (¾ mile) after Bradbourne 'Bakewell B5056 (A6)', 'Ballidon, Longcliffe'

15 L after 1 km (¾ mile) 'Ballidon 1, Parwich 1½'

16 L at triangular junction 'Parwich ¾'

17 Bear L after entering Parwich, pass church and green on your right

18 Bear R at three-way junction 'Newhaven 4, Buxton 15¼', then bear L facing Parwich Hall

19 R at T-j ('Buxton A515, Newhaven 1½, Sterndale Moor 9') then L after 150 m (yd) (NS)

20 Go through gate L just before overbridge, up steps on side of embankment and R onto Tissington Trail

two pages

Take care not to mistake the faded yellow line of the national park boundary for the solid yellow line of the route

The Wye Valley and Chatsworth

A fairly short ride, packed full of interest, over country that deserves some time for exploration. The stretch from Miller's Dale to Monsal Head through the upper Wye Valley is delightful. Chatsworth and the return through the woods to Bakewell provide further sources of pleasure.

Start

Bakewell Tourist Information Office, Market Place

P Extensive parking in Bakewell (often busy)

Distance and grade

38 km (24 miles)
Easy/moderate

Terrain

A variety of terrains is encountered. The route from Bakewell to Shelton and Taddington needs an effort. There is a climb up the northern flank of the valley, followed by a sharp descent and another strenuous climb to Monsal Head. The off-road route between Chatsworth and Haddon is not difficult, but may need care when wet or muddy

▲ *Miller's and Monsal Dales from Monsal Head*

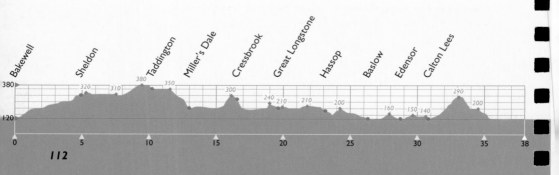

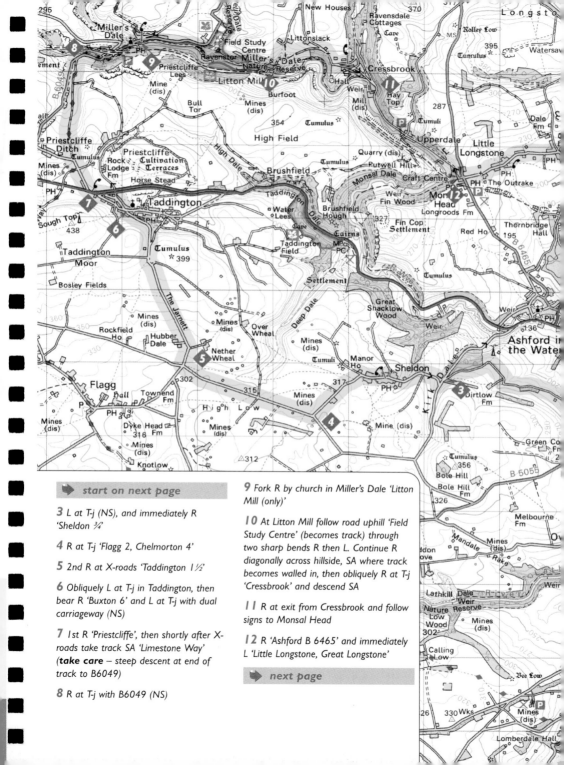

➡ start on next page

3 L at T-j (NS), and immediately R 'Sheldon ¾'

4 R at T-j 'Flagg 2, Chelmorton 4'

5 2nd R at X-roads 'Taddington 1½'

6 Obliquely L at T-j in Taddington, then bear R 'Buxton 6' and L at T-j with dual carriageway (NS)

7 1st R 'Priestcliffe', then shortly after X-roads take track SA 'Limestone Way' (**take care** – steep descent at end of track to B6049)

8 R at T-j with B6049 (NS)

9 Fork R by church in Miller's Dale 'Litton Mill (only)'

10 At Litton Mill follow road uphill 'Field Study Centre' (becomes track) through two sharp bends R then L. Continue R diagonally across hillside, SA where track becomes walled in, then obliquely R at T-j 'Cressbrook' and descend SA

11 R at exit from Cressbrook and follow signs to Monsal Head

12 R 'Ashford B 6465' and immediately L 'Little Longstone, Great Longstone'

➡ next page

Monsal Dale 12

Monsal Dale is the part of the Wye Valley that stretches to the south of the old railway viaduct on your right as you climb up to Monsal Head. There is no road through this part of the valley, only footpaths, but they give access to marvellous scenery. Litton and Cressbrook Mills took pauper apprentices from London in the 18th and 19th-centuries. It seems that those who were sent to Cressbrook found conditions less Dickensian than their colleagues at Litton Mill

Haddon Hall 20/21

A romantic, English country house above the left bank of the River Wye and its meadows with a wonderful view south towards Over Haddon that seemingly hangs in the air some 150 m (500 ft) higher. The house dates from the 12th to 16th-centuries. It was restored with an eye on historical accuracy earlier this century and contains much material from medieval and Tudor times

Refreshments

Plenty of choice in **Bakewell**
Cock and Pullett PH, **Sheldon**
Waterloo PH (just off route on A6 west of **Taddington**)
Angler's Rest PH, **Miller's Dale**
Refreshments near **Litton Mill** and **Cressbrook Mill**
Tea rooms and Inn, **Monsal Head**
Pack Horse Inn, **Little Longstone**
The Crispin, **Great Longstone**
Eyre Arms, **Hassop**
Devonshire Arms, **Pilsley**
Tea rooms at **Edensor**
Cafe at garden centre, **Calton Lees**
Tea rooms at Haddon Hall for visitors to the house

Matlock 13 km (8 miles) from Bakewell Buxton 10 km (6 miles) from Taddington

1 From Bakewell Tourist Information Centre along Bridge Street towards Rutland Arms, L at roundabout Matlock Street and immediately R King Street ('B5055 Monyash 5')

2 2nd R uphill 'Ashford 2'

 previous page

13 L Church Lane 'Rowland, Hassop' in Great Longstone

14 Obliquely L at T-j in Hassop 'Hathersage B6001', then 1st R 'Baslow 2'

15 R at T-j (NS) then R at T-j with A619 (in effect SA) 'Bakewell A619, Rowsley B6012' 'Chatsworth'

16 SA for off-road route

17 Fork R 'Calton Lees, Car Park'. Pass car park and bear R. Cross drives to left and right and continue SA up unsealed track (NS). Through gateway with notice to cyclists, then zigzag R and L uphill and SA between two houses onto unsurfaced track

18 Through field gate and turn L (from here the route is well waymarked) along edge of field. Through gateway L along track (bearing L then R) and turn obliquely L where a gap in the turf resembling a plough-marked footpath leaves the track. Climb towards gate ahead

19 Through two field gates, then R along wall and bear L on grassy section of track. Through gateposts, then L (the path is both waymarked and well defined, but at a bend R becomes wider and softer). Turn sharp L beside Haddon Estate Wildlife Trail board, then shortly fork R downhill (waymark sign) and follow clearly defined path to meeting of four bridleways

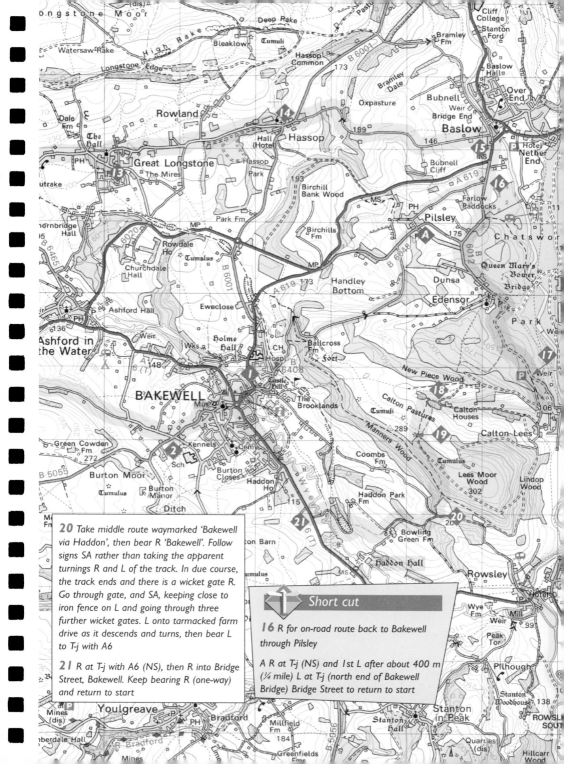

20 Take middle route waymarked 'Bakewell via Haddon', then bear R 'Bakewell'. Follow signs SA rather than taking the apparent turnings R and L of the track. In due course, the track ends and there is a wicket gate R. Go through gate, and SA, keeping close to iron fence on L and going through three further wicket gates. L onto tarmacked farm drive as it descends and turns, then bear L to T-j with A6

21 R at T-j with A6 (NS), then R into Bridge Street, Bakewell. Keep bearing R (one-way) and return to start

Short cut

16 R for on-road route back to Bakewell through Pilsley

A R at T-j (NS) and 1st L after about 400 m (¼ mile) L at T-j (north end of Bakewell Bridge) Bridge Street to return to start

21 *From Matlock to Monyash*

A fine ride offering a variety of cycling. First the route runs upstream, above the Derwent and Wye valleys, then along the Monsal Trail. The return takes you over the open landscape of the White Peak plateau, giving extensive views of distant horizons, while passing through old mining villages.

▼ *Sheepwash Bridge, Ashford in the Water*

Start

Matlock Station (When Peak Railway is running to Darley Dale from Matlock Riverside – signed from Matlock BR – the section between Matlock and Darley Bridge could be missed out. Leave Darley Dale station, turn R across level crossing and join the route at instruction 3)

P Free long-stay car park adjoining Matlock Station

Distance and grade

48 km (30 miles)

Moderate

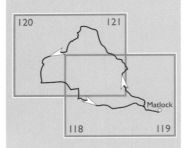

120	121
118	119

Matlock

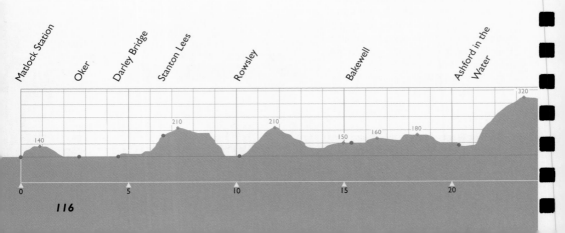

Matlock Station · Oker · Darley Bridge · Stanton Lees · Rowsley · Bakewell · Ashford in the Water

140 · 210 · 210 · 150 · 160 · 180 · 320

0   5   10   15   20

Terrain

Effort is required for the climbs out of the valleys – from Rowsley to Stanton Lees and particularly up Kirk Dale

Nearest railway

Matlock

Places of interest

Darley Dale *3*
12th-century St Helen's Church has stained glass by Burne-Jones and the weatherworn remains of a great yew tree in its graveyard. There is a handsome 15th-century bridge across the Derwent. Just off the A6 are the Derbyshire Museum and Art Centre and the Working Carriage Museum

Stanton *4/5 (just off the route)*
Stanton Moor has more than seventy barrows, cairns and other ancient relics, including the Nine Ladies – a prehistoric standing-stone circle. There are other farm houses from the 16th and 17th-centuries

Arbor Low *16 (signed R after about 1 km (¾ mile))*
The major neolithic site of the Peak and dubbed the 'Stonehenge of the North', Arbor Low is 46 limestone slabs lying on a circular bank surrounded by a ditch over 240 m (800 ft) in circumference and four stones in the centre. Access is by concessionary path, and there is an honesty box. There are many other prehistoric remains in the vicinity

Refreshments

Country Gallery at **Caudwell's Mill**
Plenty of choice in **Bakewell**
Cottage Tea Room and shops at **Ashford in the Water**
Bull's Head PH, **Monyash**
Cafe and PH at **Elton**
Pubs in **Winster**
Plenty of choice in **Matlock**

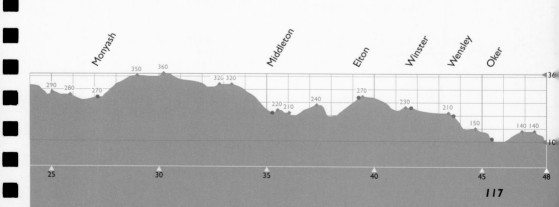

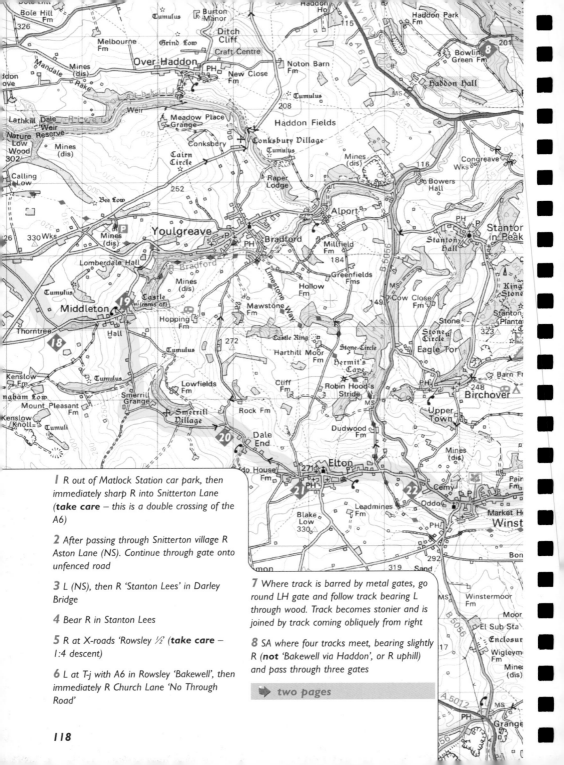

1 R out of Matlock Station car park, then immediately sharp R into Snitterton Lane (**take care** – this is a double crossing of the A6)

2 After passing through Snitterton village R Aston Lane (NS). Continue through gate onto unfenced road

3 L (NS), then R 'Stanton Lees' in Darley Bridge

4 Bear R in Stanton Lees

5 R at X-roads 'Rowsley ½' (**take care** – 1:4 descent)

6 L at T-j with A6 in Rowsley 'Bakewell', then immediately R Church Lane 'No Through Road'

7 Where track is barred by metal gates, go round LH gate and follow track bearing L through wood. Track becomes stonier and is joined by track coming obliquely from right

8 SA where four tracks meet, bearing slightly R (**not** 'Bakewell via Haddon', or R uphill) and pass through three gates

➡ two pages

18 L at T-j 'Middleton ½'

19 Sharp R in Middleton (NS) and pass church on L

20 R at T-j (NS) (**take care**)

21 SA through Elton village

22 SA at X-roads with B5056 'Winster B5057'

23 **Easy to miss** – half-way down descent from Wensley towards Darley Bridge, fork R 'Oker, Snitterton'. Through Oker and follow reverse of outward route back to start

⚠ *Take care not to mistake the faded yellow line of the national park boundary for the solid yellow line of the route*

7 Where track is barred by metal gates, go round LH gate and follow track bearing L through wood. Track becomes stonier and is joined by track coming obliquely from right

8 SA where four tracks meet, bearing slightly R (**not** 'Bakewell via Haddon', or R uphill) and pass through three gates

9 R up path on side of embankment after old railway viaduct, past wooden gate (marked 2 on gatepost) and L onto Monsal Trail

10 In about 5 km (3 miles) go under overbridge soon after passing footpath (signed across trail) and enter Great Longstone Station. Carry bike up steps on far RH side of bridge, then R at exit onto road (this is the last cycle access for the Monsal Trail)

11 SA at X-roads, then bear L into Ashford in the Water (NS) and L again at T-j 'Bakewell, Matlock' (in effect SA) along main street

12 Where road bears L, enter bay marked 'Buses Only' and **walk** SA across footbridge onto A6. On road R, then 1st L (NS)

13 R at T-j at summit (NS)

14 1st L (NS)

15 L at T-j 'Monyash', then SA at X-roads into Rake Road and bear R 'Newhaven 4, Youlgreave 6' ('White Peak scenic route')

16 L 'Youlgreave, Lathkilldale', 'Arbor Low', 'White Peak scenic route' just before T-j with A515

17 R after 3 km (1¾ miles) 'White Peak scenic route' and SA at X-roads 'Middleton 1'

18 L at T-j 'Middleton ½'

19 Sharp R in Middleton (NS) and pass church on left

previous page

Rowarth, the Etherow and Werneth Low

A short ride exploring the land to the west of the A624. The countryside is often very quiet, but the roads from Marple to Mottram can be busier than their width suggests. There are good views between Simmondley and Charlesworth, from Monks' Road and from Werneth Low.

Start

Glossop Station

P Several public car parks in Glossop. Etherow Country Park at Compstall

Distance and grade

34 km (21 miles)

Moderate/ strenuous

Terrain

The route ascends some mighty, though not too lengthy, hills: Monks' Road from Charlesworth and from

Refreshments

Several pubs, cafes and shops in **Glossop**
Moorfield Arms, **Rowarth**
Hare and Hounds, **Mill Brow**
Cafe at Etherow Valley Country Park
Pubs in **Mottram in Longdendale**

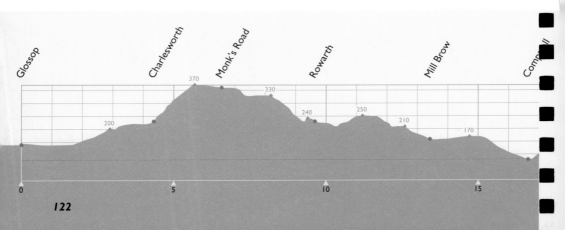

Compstall to Werneth Low. The descent of Apple Street (17–18) is also steep and will need care. Another steep rise to cross the River Etherow between Broadbottom and Charlesworth, however, there are long stretches of more gentle descent

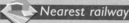
Nearest railway

Broadbottom, Dinting, Glossop and Marple

Places of interest

Compstall 10
A former mill village. Nearby Etherow Country Park stretches north for about 1 km (¾ mile) along both wooded banks of the Etherow from the mill pool. The park has much of interest in natural history and there are several trails to walk

Werneth Low 13
The obelisk and the surrounding land form the War Memorial of the former Borough of Hyde. There are panoramic views in almost all directions, across the Cheshire Plain into Wales, as well as towards the Peak and Pennines. Facilities include a visitor centre and cafe, open at weekends

Mottram 18
The artist LS Lowry lived here. There is a conservation area, and a prominent maypole-like structure at the crossing into Church Row

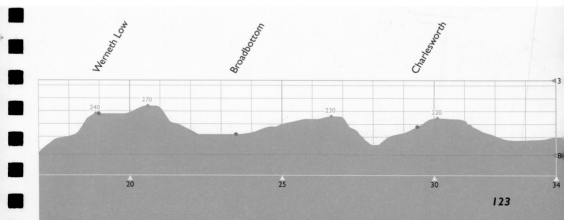

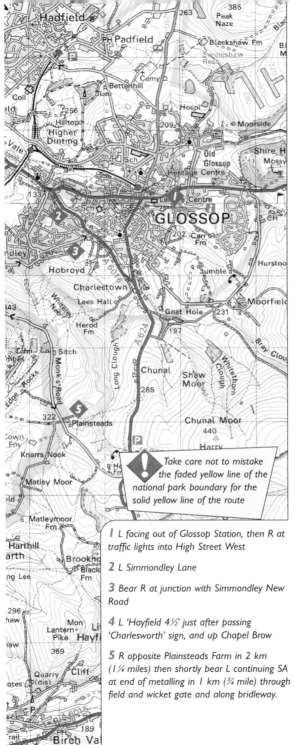

Across miniature ford and uphill (**not** L through gate along footpath) to second wicket gate, where L along farm drive into Rowarth and SA, passing car park on left

6 R at T-j 'New Mills'

7 L at T-j 'New Mills', then immediately R (with Moorfield Arms PH on your left) and continue for 3 km (2 miles) always bearing R

8 R at T-j with A626, then immediately L Cote Green Road

9 R at T-j Cote Green Lane

10 R at T-j with B6104 (NS)

11 Drop to crossing of River Etherow, then climb for 1 km (¾ mile)

12 R Coulishaw Lane (NS) at triangular junction at brow of hill, then bear R in 2 km (1¼ mile) at further triangular junction at top of hill (**take care** – busy road)

13 L, then immediately R and bear R again into Werneth Low Road at off-set X-roads (in effect SA and follow road markings)

14 Bear R (steak house ahead) past 'Unsuitable for Motors' sign and down steep, concrete-surfaced track (**take care** – there are transverse drainage channels and a tight LH bend on the steep section)

15 R at T-j with Mottram Old Road

16 2nd L Chapman Road, then R at T-j Hattersley Road East

17 R at T-j, then SA at X-roads (traffic lights) into Ashworth Lane

18 SA into Church Brow at X-roads in Mottram-in-Longdendale

19 L at T-j, then under railway bridge into Lower Market Street, cross River Etherow and bear R uphill on Long Lane

20 L at T-j in Charlesworth, then immediately R into Town Lane '3 tonne limit' bearing L into High Lane 'Simmondley 1, Glossop 2'. Follow High Lane, bearing L where it becomes Simmondley Lane, returning to Glossop Station by reverse of outward route

Take care not to mistake the faded yellow line of the national park boundary for the solid yellow line of the route

1 L facing out of Glossop Station, then R at traffic lights into High Street West

2 L Simmondley Lane

3 Bear R at junction with Simmondley New Road

4 L 'Hayfield 4½' just after passing 'Charlesworth' sign, and up Chapel Brow

5 R opposite Plainsteads Farm in 2 km (1¼ miles) then shortly bear L continuing SA at end of metalling in 1 km (¾ mile) through field and wicket gate and along bridleway.

Notes

Notes

Useful addresses

British Cycling Federation

National Cycling Centre
Stuart Street
Manchester M11 4DQ
0870 871 2000
www.bcf.uk.com

The BCF co-ordinates and promotes an array of cycle sports and cycling in general. They are a good first point of contact if you want to find out more about how to get involved in cycling. The website provides information on upcoming cycle events and competitions.

CTC (Cyclists Touring Club)

Cotterell House
69 Meadrow
Godalming
Surrey GU7 3HS
01483 417217
www.ctc.org.uk

Britain's largest cycling organisation, promoting recreational and utility cycling. The CTC provides touring and technical advice, legal aid and insurance, and campaigns to improve facilities and opportunities for all cyclists. The website provides details of campaigns and routes and has an online application form.

The London Cycling Campaign

Unit 228
30 Great Guildford Street
London SE1 0HS
020 7928 7220
www.lcc.org.uk

The LCC promotes cycling in London by providing services for cyclists and by campaigning for more facilities for cyclists. Membership of the LCC provides the following benefits: London Cyclist magazine, insurance, legal advice, workshops, organised rides, discounts in bike shops and much more. You can join the LCC on its website.

Sustrans

Head Office
Crown House
37-41 Prince Street
Bristol BS1 4PS
General information line: 0117 929 0888
www.sustrans.org.uk

A registered charity, Sustrans designs and builds systems for sustainable transport. It is best known for its transformation of old railway lines into safe, traffic-free routes for cyclists and pedestrians and wheelchair users. Sustrans is developing the 13,000 km (8000 mile) National Cycle Network on traffic-calmed minor roads and traffic-free paths, to be completed by the year 2005 with major funding from the Millennium Commission.

Veteran Cycle Club

Membership Secretary
31 Yorke Road
Croxley Green
Rickmansworth
Herts WD3 3DW
www.v-cc.org.uk

A very active club, the VCC is concerned with the history and restoration of veteran cycles. Members enjoy organised rides and receive excellent publications relating to cycle history and club news.